Also by Melanie Scherencel Bockmann:

Just Plane Crazy
UnRapped

To order, call **1-800-765-6955.**

Visit us at **www.reviewandherald.com** for
information on other Review and Herald® products.

In the Shadow of the Mob

"Caught between two worlds,
Carl would have to choose one."

Melanie Scherencel Bockmann

REVIEW AND HERALD® PUBLISHING ASSOCIATION
Since 1861 | www.reviewandherald.com

Copyright © 2011 by Review and Herald® Publishing Association

Published by Review and Herald® Publishing Association, Hagerstown, MD
21741-1119

Review and Herald® titles may be purchased in bulk for educational, business,
fund-raising, or sales promotional use. For information, e-mail SpecialMarkets@
reviewandherald.com.

The Review and Herald® Publishing Association publishes biblically based materials
for spiritual, physical, and mental growth and Christian discipleship.

The author assumes full responsibility for the accuracy of all facts and quotations as
cited in this book.

Bible texts in this book are from the *Holy Bible, New International Version*.
Copyright © 1973, 1978, 1984, 2011 by Biblica, Inc. Used by permission. All
rights reserved worldwide.

This book was
Edited by Kalie Kelch
Copyedited by Jeremy J. Johnson
Cover designed by Brandon Reese
Cover art by thinkstock.com
Typeset: Bembo 11/13

PRINTED IN U.S.A.

15   14   13   12   11   5   4   3   2   1

Library of Congress Cataloging-in-Publication Data
Bockmann, Melanie Scherencel, 1974- .
  In the shadow of the mob / Melanie Scherencel Bockmann.
       p. cm.
1. Rodriguez, Carl—Childhood and youth—Juvenile literature. 2. Seventh-Day
Adventist converts—United States—Biography—Juvenile literature. 3. Children of
criminals—United States—Biography—Juvenile literature. 4. Mafia—United
States—Juvenile literature. I. Title.
  BX6189.R63B63 2011
  286.7'32092—dc22
  [B]
                                              2011016355

ISBN 978-0-8280-2583-6

CHAPTER I

Carl wiped the sweat off his forehead and squinted into the hot afternoon sun. It was a perfect day for baseball, and his team had won again. The streaks of dirt on the front of his uniform and the scrape on his arm were proof of the base he'd stolen to help solidify his team's win—a slick competitive move that had earned him a half-dozen congratulatory slaps on the back from his teammates. But there was something missing from his perfect day—his dad. If only his dad had been able to come watch him slide into home.

"Hey, Carl!" his friend Bobby called. "Where's your dad today?"

"Couldn't make it," Carl said. "He had to work."

"Too bad." Bobby took his hat off and waved. "Well, see ya!" he said as he ran to where his own dad stood next to the bleachers.

Carl watched as Bobby's dad smiled and patted him on the back, and then Carl turned away. His dad was rarely able to attend his baseball games, so he wasn't surprised that his dad wasn't there. What did surprise him was the disappointment he felt in his chest and the way the cheers of the crowd sounded empty without his dad's voice joining in.

It's no big deal. I don't need him here. Besides, I should be used to it by now, he thought, irritated at himself for caring. He pumped his fist into his baseball glove a couple of times and tried hard to focus on the fact that he and his teammates had won, and it was time to celebrate.

Carl knew his dad expected him to be a man about his feelings and keep his demeanor strong. "Our family is different, Carl. We can't let other people know what goes on with us, especially with me. If people found out, I could go to jail for a long time. Or worse. You understand that, right, son?"

"Yeah, Dad, I know," Carl would say. He had always known his dad didn't have a choice when it came to missing his baseball games or other family events. Nothing got in the way of his dad's job—not even family. He also knew his dad would make it up to him as soon as he could.

Most of Carl's friends' dads worked in factories or offices in the city, but his dad had a different kind of job—a job Carl and his family knew better than to talk about. It was a secret the entire family had gotten really good at keeping. While they told people his dad worked at a local hospital and did carpentry work, those jobs were only a cover-up for his real occupation: Carl's dad worked for a powerful and dangerous system of organized crime known and feared throughout New York City and beyond—the Italian Mafia.

Carl's dad protected him, his mother, and his brother, Angel, from the details of his involvement with the Mafia. It was safer that way. Besides, his father had adopted the Mob's strict code of silence, and he had to be very careful with his words. The less he said, the better.

Even though Carl didn't understand all the details, he knew that whatever his dad did for the Mafia earned him a lot of money. From the outside, no one would have known that they were anything but a normal, middle-class Puerto Rican family, which is exactly the way Carl's dad wanted it to be. For the time being, Carl's family lived in the projects in the Bronx—his dad felt it was best not to give anyone a reason to wonder where the family's influx of money was coming from.

"Our home in the projects is only temporary. Eventually, someday, we will move into a nice, big house out in the country somewhere," his dad promised. "Just be patient until the time is right."

Carl could hardly wait. On the outside he was like the other inner-city boys his age, toughened by experience and street-savvy, but sometimes as he walked the few blocks between home and school, dodging traffic and people, he would let his mind wander and imagine what it would be like to live in a place with fresh air and wide-open spaces. *I guess I must be a country boy on the inside,* he thought.

Though his dad chose to keep their living arrangements modest and inconspicuous, the boys' education was a different story. His dad had enrolled them in St. Jerome School—the most expensive school in the area. The boys also had everything else they needed or wanted. New electronic gadgets, expensive shoes and clothes, weekend events with their friends. It didn't matter how much something cost; if Carl wanted it, he got it.

One time when Carl was in the car with his dad, he had noticed a brown paper bag under the seat.

He'd pulled it out and looked inside, and what he saw made his mouth go dry. The bag had contained hundreds of $1,000 bills.

"Dad! Is this real? Where did this come from?" Carl had asked.

His dad had quickly snatched it away and stashed it back in its hiding place. "Son, you must keep this between us. Yes, the money is real, but I can't tell you where it came from or why I have it. I have to be able to trust you. Someday, if you do what I tell you to do, I'll explain."

Carl hadn't asked any more questions, but he'd known the bag of money had something to do with the Mafia. Whatever his dad was doing for the Mob was making him a lot of cash, and Carl was intrigued. He hoped someday his father would trust him enough to tell him his secrets.

The money and his dad's Mafia involvement came at a cost, however, and Carl was personally aware of what that meant. Though his family rarely mentioned it, Carl knew that his aunts and uncles wanted little to do with them because of his dad's Mafia ties. After moving from Puerto Rico to the United States, all of his dad's siblings had taken legitimate jobs, and they now lived modestly in average neighborhoods. They definitely didn't approve of Carl's dad's illegal activities. One time Carl had even overheard his aunts and uncles talking about his dad and what they called his "blood money."

"Blood money," he had thought. *I wonder what they mean by "blood money."*

As a result of the strained relationship, Carl and

his family did not always feel welcome when they were invited to his cousins' birthday parties, holiday celebrations, and summer barbecues. And when it came to the rest of his extended family, Carl's family mostly felt like outcasts. Sometimes he felt embarrassed and angry about the feeling of isolation, and sometimes he just felt sad. But for the most part, his life was just the way he wanted it.

Regardless of his disappointment that day after the baseball game, by the time the other families had picked up their blankets, popcorn, and sodas to leave, he had made up his mind not to let his dad's absence bother him. Besides, not much could ruin a good day at the ballpark.

"Hey, want to go get a soda at the store across the street?" Carl asked his teammate Daniel as they gathered the baseball equipment after the game. "I've got money. It's on me."

"Wish I could," Daniel replied with a shake of his head. "But I promised my mom I'd come home right after the game. She gets crazy if she doesn't know where I am."

"No problem," Carl shrugged. "I understand. I guess I'll see you at tomorrow's practice, then."

Carl draped a loose arm over each end of the baseball bat balanced on his shoulders and began walking by himself across the vacant lot toward the little corner store. His cleats clacked on the asphalt, and he kicked a small stone that skittered across the sidewalk into the grass. He thought about what he'd do when he got home—maybe play some video games or watch TV or ride his bike.

"Carl."

Carl looked up when he heard the voice, but he didn't see anyone. Cautiously he peeked around some parked cars to see if someone was hiding behind them, but there was no one there.

"Carl, it's going to be all right."

Carl looked up and bristled with irritation. "All right—who's there? You'd better show yourself. What are you talking about? What's going to be all right?"

Someone was definitely messing with him, and when he found out who that person was, he was going to—

"Carl," the voice said again, "some things in your life are going to change, but it's going to be all right."

Carl looked everywhere for the source of the voice, but he was alone in the vacant lot. A strange feeling of panic crept over him, and he hurried toward the store. He never backed down from a fight, but he didn't like the anxious feeling that tickled the hairs on the back of his neck. *Can't fight what I can't see,* Carl thought, looking back over his shoulder to see if someone was following him. Each time he turned around, it appeared that no one else was there, and that made him angry.

The little bell on the door jingled as he walked in. He nodded to the cashier and went to the refrigerator cases to find his favorite soft drink. Even the cold air that enveloped him as he opened the glass doors couldn't help him shake the strange feeling that he was not alone.

I wonder if that was God, he thought as he passed

his money to the cashier and twisted the top off of his soda. Carl vaguely knew about God from attending St. Jerome School and hearing the priests talk about Him, but he didn't understand much about who He was or why He'd be interested in a dusty kid on his way to get a cold drink after a baseball game. It didn't make sense. Plus, it made him nervous to think about his life changing.

"I like my life the way it is," Carl said out loud when he got back outside. He wondered if the voice heard him. "I don't want it to change." This time there was no response.

What Carl didn't know was that his life had already started to change, and before long, nothing would ever be the same.

CHAPTER 2

Days passed, but Carl did not hear the voice again, causing him to wonder if he had somehow imagined it. Gradually he forgot about it altogether, and life went on as usual. Between school and baseball, Carl fell into a normal routine and forgot about the mystery voice who had said his life would be changing.

"Hey, has anyone seen my baseball bat?" Carl called to his teammates as he looked around the dugout. The game was over, and for some reason his favorite bat was missing. "I know I put it right here, and now it's gone."

"If it's gone, I have an idea of what might have happened to it," Bobby said. "I saw that kid José hanging around here right after the game ended. Maybe he took it."

"Why would you think that?" Carl asked. He peeked under the bench in the dugout, still searching.

"He's not a member of our league or anything, but he kind of hangs out whenever there's a game. He's been known to walk off with stuff that's not his. He has a reputation."

Carl felt his blood rushing and the familiar energy of adrenaline kicking in. He wasn't the type to let some kid walk off with his favorite bat. "I'll take care of this," Carl decided out loud as he tossed his baseball and mitt into his bag. "José who? Where does this kid live?"

"Oh, no, you don't," Bobby said, shaking his head as he packed up his own gear. "Carl, listen. I know you. I know you have no problem getting in somebody's face if they deserve it. But not this time. Trust me, this kid is trouble. You don't want to mess with him."

"Why not?"

"Stealing isn't the only thing he has a reputation for. He fights dirty. Everybody knows it, and nobody messes with him."

Carl smirked. "Nobody except Carl Rodriguez," he said. "Come on, tell me where he lives. I'll show you how I handle this situation. I'm not leaving without my bat. Period."

"This is a bad, bad idea, Carl." Bobby was visibly worried, but after some encouragement, he reluctantly led Carl several blocks away to the building where José lived.

Carl straightened his shoulders and knocked on the door. When the door opened, a woman answered. "Hello," she said.

"Is José around? I need to talk to him," Carl said.

"Oh, my son is not home," the woman said. "I don't know when he will be back. You could try later. Or I could tell him you stopped by."

"No, thank you," he said politely. "But maybe you can help me. I think your son may have borrowed my bat, and I need to get it back. Would you mind checking around for me?"

Carl and Bobby watched while José's mom opened a closet door and rummaged around a little.

When she emerged, she was holding Carl's bat. "Is this it?" she asked.

"Yes, thank you," Carl said as she handed it to him. "I'll just go ahead and take it now. Be sure to let him know I came and got it."

"OK, I'll tell him," José's mom said as she closed the door.

As they walked away from the building and into the alleyway, Bobby still looked worried. "Carl, why did you tell her that? You know you are in for a fight when José finds out what you did."

"So?" Carl said. "Let him try. It'd be entertaining." It was just the kind of challenge he was in the mood for, and he almost hoped José would confront him about it. He didn't have to wait long.

"Hey, you!"

Carl and Bobby turned around just in time to see José and a group of his friends coming down the small street.

"What do you think you're doing with my bat?" José demanded. He walked up to Carl and put his face up close to Carl's as his friends gathered around. Carl and Bobby were clearly outnumbered, but Carl wasn't concerned.

"Sorry, dude, you're on your own," Bobby whispered. He backed up a few steps, then turned and ran away, leaving Carl to face the gang of kids alone.

Carl didn't flinch as he looked José in the eyes. "It's not your bat, José. It's my bat."

"You calling me a liar?" José said. It was a challenge, and Carl knew it. He stepped in closer. "I said, you calling me a liar?"

Not wanting to throw the first punch, Carl started to walk away, but José had other plans. He moved a step to block Carl's path and spit on the sidewalk. "I don't think so."

José's friends laughed, and Carl felt his temper turn red-hot. In a flash he turned and hit José squarely in the jaw. He knew the fight was on, and he was ready. He clenched his fists in anticipation of José's reaction.

It only took a second for José's face to melt from surprise to fury. A moment later Carl remembered what Bobby had said about Jose's reputation for fighting dirty, because before Carl could make another move, José whipped a knife out of his pants and flicked the blade open, pointing the tip at Carl's belly. He could feel the sharp edge through his T-shirt, and he forced himself to breathe in short gasps.

I've gone too far this time, he thought. *I'm going to lose my life over a baseball bat.*

Carl swallowed hard as he thought about his mother and father and how they would react to the news when someone showed up at their front door to tell them their oldest son had been the victim of a stabbing. He thought about his twin brother, Angel, sleeping alone in their room without him. Regret and fear stirred inside him as he waited for José's next move.

I don't want to die, Carl silently pleaded. *I'm afraid to die.*

With José's reputation, he figured he was only a moment away from having a knife plunged deep into his stomach.

CHAPTER 3

Carl felt tiny dots of sweat sting his pores as he looked into José's triumphant eyes. Even if he could somehow survive the initial thrust of José's knife, he was still outnumbered four to one, and weaponless. He fought to stay calm. Was there anyone watching? Would there be any witnesses to his murder, or would he die alone on the street?

Before another thought could enter his mind, two men suddenly stepped in front of Carl. A Black man and a White man, both very tall and ripped with muscles, stood between him and José. Carl blinked in surprise. He didn't remember seeing them anywhere on the street when the fight had started.

It's like they appeared out of thin air, Carl thought.

"When I say 'run,' I want you to run," the Black man told him.

When Carl heard the word "run," he turned and sprinted. He ran block after block, putting considerable distance between him and José. When he finally stopped to catch his breath, his lungs burned and his leg muscles felt like jelly.

"What just happened?" he wondered out loud. He looked behind him to make sure José and his friends hadn't followed. He relaxed when he realized he was alone.

Who were those men? Where did they come from?

Carl's brain was working overtime trying to piece all the events together from the beginning of the fight to his mysterious rescue, but it had all happened so quickly. He realized that in all the commotion he hadn't even seen their faces.

Knowing that he had almost been a New York City statistic made Carl feel sober and cautious. He knew he possessed a bold fearlessness and an aggressive temper, but today those traits had almost cost him his life. That is, until two men appeared and saved him.

Were they angels? Carl thought. That was the only explanation he could think of. He'd seen paintings of angels in the books at St. Jerome, and they usually had wings and halos, unlike the two muscle-bound bodyguards who had intervened for him. But the more Carl thought about it, the more he was sure that the men who had protected him must have been angels sent by God. The only question was . . . why?

★★★

As Carl expected, a couple of weeks later his dad made up for his game-day absence by taking Carl and his brother out to the field to play softball with some of his dad's friends. Carl didn't always feel comfortable around his dad's friends. He knew they did drugs and drank alcohol, and the more intoxicated they became, the more aggressive they seemed.

Carl took a few practice swings with the bat while he watched his father and his friends tip their beer cans and laugh loudly.

"Angel, you take first base. Carl, you cover third,"

his dad called out to them, motioning with the beer can still in his hand. "Don't let anything by you—got it?"

I'm never going to drink alcohol or do drugs, Carl thought. It seemed to Carl that alcohol always caused problems. His parents' fights usually happened when they'd both been drinking. Carl just didn't see the point.

While he didn't like the loud, unstable atmosphere of drinking and drugs, Carl did love softball, and the game was a good one, with both teams competing hard and fast against each other. Carl put every ounce of energy and focus he had on hitting the ball into the weak spot in the outfield and snagging runners when he was covering his base. Even so, the teams were evenly matched, and the score remained close.

As the game continued, Carl noticed that his dad seemed to be drinking more than usual, and he was even staggering a little bit.

"Did you notice how much Dad is drinking?" Carl whispered to Angel.

Angel nodded. "I'm surprised he can even stand up at all. With what they've been drinking, I'm surprised *any* of them can stand up, much less hit the ball!"

Carl tried to work out the uneasy feeling by punching his fist into his glove and getting back into the game.

Near the end of the final inning the game was tied. With two outs against his team already, Carl's dad was up to bat. Just before he stepped up to the plate, he handed Carl his beer can.

"Carl, I didn't tell you this before," his dad whispered, "but there's money riding on this game."

"You placed bets on the game?" Carl whispered back. "How much?"

"Trust me. It's a lot," his dad said. "The winning team takes it all."

"Come on, Cano, get up to bat!" one of the guys yelled.

"If he can even find the plate!" another guy joked. "He's been drinking like a fish! Strike him out!"

"Look at what's inside the beer can," Carl's dad whispered with a wink.

"Look inside the beer can?" Carl repeated, confused. "Why?"

Everyone on the field relaxed as Carl's dad staggered up to the plate with the bat. The pitcher bent down, received the signal from the catcher, nodded, and wound up an easy pitch in Carl's dad's direction. As he threw the first pitch, however, Carl's dad straightened up and hit it hard and square over everyone's heads. The outfielders had not expected him to hit anything in his drunken state, and they scrambled unsuccessfully for the ball as Carl's dad rounded the bases.

"He's not even drunk," Carl whispered. He looked down into the beer can he was holding and realized it was full of water. His dad had tricked the opposing team.

As his dad rounded third, Carl realized what his father had done. He had pretended to drink during the whole game to make everyone think he was intoxicated so they would be unprepared. Instead, he was playing fully sober. As he scored the winning run for the team, his dad gave him a high five. "Son, that's how you do it. You play with your head, not just with your muscles."

Carl thought about his dad's ability to be deceptive and convincing—he was sure those were qualities that made him good at his Mafia job. He had wondered how his dad had become involved with the Italian Mafia, since he wasn't Italian. Though he looked Italian with his light skin and strong facial features, Carl's dad was Puerto Rican. All his dad would tell him was that he had impressed some friends and that had paved the way for him to be involved with the Mob.

A few days later Carl's dad took him aside. "Son, I want you to come with me," he said. "I want to show you a few things. But this is between us, you understand? You tell no one. Not your mother, not Angel, no one."

"OK," Carl said, following his dad out to the car. "But where are we going?"

"You'll see," his dad said. "I want to tell you something. There are some qualities a man in my position needs. I think I see those same qualities in you, and that's why I'm letting you in on some things. This could be beneficial to your future."

Carl couldn't hold back a proud grin. "What qualities?"

His dad smiled and clamped a hand on Carl's shoulder. "You've got to be sharp and know how to defend yourself and take care of business. And you've got to know how to keep your mouth shut. People who don't keep their mouths shut disappear. Do you understand, son?"

Carl didn't need to ask what happened to the

people who "disappeared." He had seen news reports of Mafia-related disappearances. Sometimes the bodies were found, sometimes they weren't. He vowed that he would watch everything, but say nothing. *I'm a vault,* he thought.

Carl's dad turned the car down a street and parked outside a row of stores.

"Get ready, son," his dad said. "Remember what I said. No talking, no asking questions."

Carl got out of the car and followed his dad inside. They walked past the cashiers and the neatly stocked shelves and through a doorway in the back that opened up into a big storage area that connected all of the storefronts together. *They're all connected!* Carl thought. *I wonder why these competing stores are joined together?*

The men in the back nodded a furtive greeting at Carl's dad, and Carl stayed close behind as his father talked with each of the men, wrote down numbers, and collected cash. When they left, Carl's dad had a huge stack of bills with him. They walked straight to the car, climbed in, and closed the doors. Carl put his seat belt on while his dad started the engine. He didn't ask any questions, but it wasn't long before his dad started talking.

"It looks like those stores are competing, but they're really not. The Mob owns all of them. They're storefronts, but there's a complex operation happening behind them. It's an easy way to move money and goods without anybody asking any questions."

"Why are they connected like that in the back?" Carl finally asked.

"The police know that there is illegal activity happening there, so we have to be prepared. If the police ever raid one storefront, the goods and cash can be easily moved and locked in another segment of the storage area, and they would find nothing," Carl's dad explained.

"The Mob runs grocery stores?" Carl grinned.

His dad didn't smile. "They run this whole city, Carl. And what they don't actually operate, they collect a kind of Mob tax, which people are willing to pay to stay safe. The Mafia owns and operates grocery stores, casinos, nightclubs, construction companies, even garbage-collection companies."

"Garbage companies?" Carl laughed. "Seems like a strange choice."

"Sometimes certain things need to be disposed of," Carl's dad said carefully. "Owning the garbage company means those items can be . . . you know . . . transported without anyone else knowing about it."

Carl swallowed and remembered what his dad had said about people disappearing for breaking the code of silence. He wondered if his dad could disappear for telling him this information. He felt the heaviness of the secret and was determined to lock it away. After all, not even Mom or Angel really knew.

"What were we doing there, in the storage areas behind the storefronts?" Carl asked.

"*Números,* son," his dad said. "Numbers. It's gambling. It's illegal, but highly profitable for the Mafia. People bet $1 or $10 or $100 on the numbers. There are a high percentage of wins. When the numbers are drawn, there is a payout. We just collected the money and processed the payouts."

The wheels started turning in Carl's head as he calculated the amount of money exchanging hands.

"I know what you're thinking," his dad said. "I know you love to make money. You get crazy ideas and sell things. This is an easy way to make money."

Carl looked over at his dad.

"I took the shortcut," his dad continued. "But there is a price you pay for the shortcut. I want you to understand that."

"Dad?" Carl asked. "Is numbers the only thing you do for the Mob?"

Carl's dad fell silent. "Enough about that for now," his dad said, turning into a parking lot. "How about we go bowling?"

Carl spent the afternoon with his dad at the bowling alley. While his dad missed a lot of baseball games and family events, he made up for it by spending time with Carl and Angel when he could. And even when he couldn't be there, he always made sure his boys had plenty of money to spend. It was a trade-off. The Mob came first, and family came second—but there were plenty of perks in exchange for being second place in his dad's life.

Carl's dad didn't say anything else about his Mob activities during the next few weeks, but one day when he came home, he seemed worried. There were crease lines on his forehead, his eyes were wide, and he paced around the house restlessly.

"What's wrong, Dad?" Carl asked. When he didn't get any response, he moved closer to his dad and whispered so that his mother and brother couldn't hear. "Dad, is everything OK? Can't you just tell me what's going on? Did something go wrong? You're scaring me."

His dad moved into the other room, and Carl followed him.

"It's going to be fine," his dad said.

Carl wondered if his dad was trying to convince him, or himself.

"I made a mistake, Carl. A mistake with the numbers. I forgot to collect, and there was no cap, and now I owe them money. A lot of money."

"How much, Dad?" Carl asked. "We have some money. Maybe we can just—"

"Carl, it's more than $1 million," his dad interrupted him. His eyes were wide as he stared at his son.

"A million . . ." Carl's voice trailed off as he stared back at his dad. ". . . *dollars?*"

His dad ran fingers through his own black hair and paced back and forth in the room as though he were trying to chase down a solution.

"What are you going to do?" Carl whispered, fear rising in his stomach like thick yellow bile. He thought he might get sick.

"I've got to go take care of this," his dad said. "I don't know . . . I don't know what will happen. Whatever will be will be."

"But Dad!" Carl whispered anxiously.

"I've got to go, son."

His dad straightened his shoulders, turned, and walked out the front door. Carl resisted the urge to run after him. *Keep your mouth shut,* he told himself, trying to act normal around his mom and brother.

The secret knowledge that his dad's life might be in danger burned hotly in his brain, and as his dad disappeared down the front steps Carl knew there was a serious possibility he would never see his father again.

A million dollars? Carl thought, tears filling his eyes. *There's no way out.*

CHAPTER 4

That night as Carl lay in his bed, sleep eluded him. The evening had faded to black, and his dad was still not home. His absence didn't trigger any alarms for Carl's mother or brother. They were used to him being gone, and they knew not to ask any questions. Carl could hear his brother's deep breathing as he slept, but Carl lay flat on his back, looking up at the curtains that fluttered in the cool breeze from the open window. He strained at the night noises and tried to decipher a sound—any sound—that would indicate his dad had made it home safe.

What if he doesn't come home? Carl wondered, trying not to let himself think past the question.

Suddenly Carl heard keys jingle. The front door opened, and Carl could hear heavy footsteps coming down the hall. The footsteps paused outside his room, then continued on. A few minutes later Carl could hear his father's familiar snore coming from the room down the hall.

Relieved, Carl took a deep breath and turned over. At least for tonight, his father was home safe.

The next morning Carl waited patiently for an opportunity to get his dad alone so he could find out what had happened. The worry lines on his father's face had relaxed, but his father was quiet and thoughtful.

When they were finally alone, Carl worked up the courage to ask the question that hung between them. "What happened, Dad?"

"They are going to let me pay the money back," his dad said. "We have an agreement."

"A million dollars? That will take forever."

"Well, there's more to the agreement than just that," Carl's dad continued. "They have provided me a way to make even more money than I'm making now, so I can pay them back faster."

"What way?" Carl pressed.

His father shook his head. "Maybe someday I'll tell you, son. But not now. Remember when I said there was a price to pay for the shortcut? I'm paying the price."

★★★

Summer slowly cooled into fall, and Carl and Angel went back to school at St. Jerome. Carl's parents were Catholic, but they rarely attended services except on Easter and Christmas. Carl knew that his dad often went to confession, usually after he came back from a Mob assignment. The priests would tell him what he needed to do to earn forgiveness.

The whole concept of God was confusing to Carl. Though he went to Catholic school and attended Mass occasionally, he wasn't sure he believed everything he was taught.

"Angel," Carl whispered to his brother one night as they lay in their beds, "does the idea of God make sense to you?"

"What do you mean?" Angel asked in a sleepy voice.

"I guess I just don't understand it," Carl contin-

27

ued. "From what I'm learning at school, it just seems as if God and Satan somehow work together. If I do all the right things, I go to heaven and live with God forever. But if I do the wrong things, God's just going to hand me over to Satan, and I'm going to spend forever in hell with him instead."

"Yeah? So what's your point?" Angel yawned.

"Why would God have that kind of working relationship with the devil?"

"I have no idea," Angel said. "It doesn't make sense to me, either. You know what else doesn't make sense? The nuns told me that if someone is not good enough for heaven, but not bad enough for hell, they go to purgatory, and they have to wait there until someone says enough prayers for them to get out."

"I just don't get it," Carl said.

Even though he had questions and didn't understand it all, Carl began working toward his confirmation along with his classmates, and he even began training to be an altar boy so he could assist the priests. In the back of his mind Carl remembered the voice he thought belonged to God telling him his life was going to change, and he wondered what that was about. He often thought about his two guardian angels and wondered if they were with him all the time.

With homework and school activities, he was too busy to notice that his dad was spending more and more time on assignments for the Mob. He was out late at night, and sometimes when he came home, he didn't seem as though he was in the mood to talk. He would disappear into his room or sit in front of the TV and drink. All Carl knew was that when his father was home, he was relieved, even though it was increasingly obvious that things were not OK.

As the holidays drew near, Carl noticed that both of his parents were drinking more, and his father was spending more time with his drug-addicted friends. Fights erupted between his parents more often, usually over money, and Carl felt the precarious balance in his home tipping. He tried to stay in his room when they fought, but the thin walls didn't shield him from their arguments.

"Did you take money out of my wallet again?" Carl heard his father yell.

"Why do you ask?" his mother shouted back. "Do you want to throw away *more* money gambling? Yes, Cano, I know you gamble all the time."

"You think you know everything, don't you?" Carl's dad said angrily. "But all you do is sit at home and drink and smoke your life away."

"Oh, you're talking about me and my bad habits, Cano? How dare you. I know more than you think I know! I know where you've been. You can't hide everything from me. I'm your wife."

Carl sighed and tried to put his pillow over his ears. He couldn't stand to hear the fighting. He knew his father was spending more and more time gambling, and his mother numbed herself with alcohol on a daily basis. Things were getting worse.

★★★

When Christmas Eve finally arrived, it didn't seem much like Christmas at all. In addition to the lack of cheer inside Carl's home, the weather was mild, and twinkling lights hung from twiggy, snowless branches outside. Carl put his face next to the window and fogged circles onto the glass with his breath while he wondered what was going to happen in his life. Things seemed so strange. His parents seemed to be avoiding each other, which was better than the fighting, but the tension made life uncomfortable for everyone.

He continued to watch out the window as darkness fell. Most of the neighbors had retreated inside their homes to celebrate, so the sidewalks were empty. Empty, except for two tall figures walking under the streetlights carrying packages. The figures—wearing three-piece suits—turned down the walk toward Carl's house. A moment later there was a knock at the door.

"Dad!" Carl whispered loudly. "Some big Italian guys are here. They look like they're from the Secret Service or something. They're wearing suits, and they're carrying boxes."

Carl's dad quickly switched off the television and came to open the door. Carl stayed back as his father greeted the men and invited them inside.

"Merry Christmas!" one of the men said. "We've brought some gifts for your family."

Carl thought it was odd that men he had never seen before would show up with Christmas presents for the family, and he immediately wondered if there was an ulterior motive for their visit.

"This is my wife, my son Angel, and my son Carl," Carl's dad said, pointing to each of them.

They shook hands with each of them, but the men's attention rested on Carl. "So this is Carl," one of them said.

Surprised, he looked into the man's deep chocolate-colored eyes and round face. Both men seemed to be sizing him up, but Carl stood firm under their gaze.

"We've heard a lot about you, Carl," he said. "I've been told you have a bright future ahead of you. I'm pleased to finally make your acquaintance. I'm sure we'll see you again soon."

Carl looked at his dad, who nodded and smiled at him with pride. The men wished them a good night, walked down the front steps, and disappeared down the sidewalk.

When Carl opened the present with his name on it, he couldn't believe what was inside. As accustomed as he was to his dad buying him pretty much whatever he wanted, he never expected something so expensive. It was as if the gift were a message.

Do they think I will follow in my father's footsteps and work for the Mob when I get older? he wondered. It had seemed as though the main reason for their visit was to form an impression of him, and the fact that they seemed pleased with what they saw made him nervous and proud all at the same time. He remembered what his dad had said about paying the price for taking shortcuts, and he knew that someday he would have a choice to make.

CHAPTER 5

Carl cringed and closed his bedroom door, hoping to drown out the noise of his parents fighting down the hall. Carl didn't want to hear what it was about this time. It was almost always about the same things—gambling, money, drinking, and drugs—but this time Carl knew there was a new reason for the undercurrent of resentment and anger.

A few weeks before, while Carl and his dad were out running numbers, his dad had stopped by a little apartment and introduced him to a woman. Carl had seen the familiar way she smiled at him and touched him, and he had instinctively known that this woman was his father's girlfriend. Though it made him feel sick inside to know that his father was cheating on his mother, and that he was no doubt financially supporting this woman in addition to his family, Carl had held to his code of silence and hadn't said a word about it to anyone. Still, it was another piece of his life that had been rocked out of place, and he was afraid it wouldn't be long before his world came crashing down.

One day his dad called him aside again. "Carl, I'm going on an errand. I'd like you to come with me."

They drove across town into a neighborhood with sprawling lawns and extravagant homes. Before long they came to the most beautiful house Carl had ever seen. Carl stared in awe at the huge mansion, the expensive array of vehicles parked out front, and the amazing, exotic plants and garden statues that decorated the property.

As Carl and his dad stepped out of their car, some men in suits came outside. Carl could see gun holsters semi-hidden beneath their suit coats, and he immediately felt his body stiffen.

"What is this place, Dad?" he whispered. "You know these people?" He put on a calm face, but inside he wrestled with the urge to climb back into the car.

Carl's dad didn't answer; he just motioned Carl to follow him as he walked up the steps, past the men with guns, to the front door of the mansion. With his heart beating fast against his chest, Carl followed his dad inside when the door opened.

The inside of the house was even more lavish than the outside, and Carl felt as though his eyes weren't big enough to take it all in. He followed his father down a long hallway into an open room that appeared to be an office. Behind a large desk sat an older man in a three-piece suit who leaned back in his big leather chair and looked up when Carl and his dad walked in.

This must be the boss, Carl told himself, trying not to act nervous. *I can't believe my father brought me here.*

A beautiful woman in a fancy gown walked across the room and stood at the boss's side like a living piece of art. *She looks as though she could be on the cover of a magazine,* he thought, trying to avert his eyes from her gaze. The boss man hardly seemed to notice she was there.

What surprised Carl most was that the top of the boss's desk was covered with stacks of money, and Carl was so mesmerized by the towers of crisp $100 bills that he hardly heard what his dad and the man talked about. Trying not to be too obvious, he began quickly calculating how much money must be in the stacks in front of him.

Finally the boss turned his attention to Carl. He took a couple of puffs on his cigar. "Go ahead, count it."

Carl swallowed. "Really?"

The boss nodded and smiled. "Go ahead."

Carl nervously thumbed through the stacks of money on the desk, soon realizing that there must be more than $1 million there. "Wow," he whispered.

The boss man laughed and leaned forward. "Isn't it great? Carl, let me tell you something. If you have money, you can have anything you want. Anything."

Carl felt uncomfortable under the big Italian man's watchful gaze, and he felt ever more uncomfortable when he realized the thug-looking guys with guns were all watching him as well.

"We take care of each other here," the man said. "Like a family. We help each other out. Do you understand?"

Carl nodded, but he wasn't sure he really understood what the man meant, and he wasn't sure he wanted to know. He was relieved when his dad told him it was time to go.

Carl felt conflicted. The money and the house impressed him, but he also felt afraid, and he wondered if his dad had brought him because he expected Carl to follow in his footsteps. Was it worth it to live in fear? He knew there was a price tag for access to that kind of money. And so far, that lifestyle hadn't made his dad or his home life very happy.

As they climbed into the car, his dad's pant leg slid up, revealing a gun hidden underneath. Carl was stunned.

"Dad!" Carl exclaimed. "What are you doing with a gun? What exactly do you do for the Mob? Do you . . . do you kill people?"

His dad was quiet for a moment, and then he finally answered. "Don't worry about it right now, son. I'll explain it to you someday. All I want you to know right now is that there are two things you can do in life. You can work hard now—go to college, get a career, have mobility—and enjoy life later, or you can have all the fun now and pay for it for the rest of your life. It's about choices."

Carl sat in his seat and stared out the window. He knew in his heart that things were changing, just as the strange voice he had heard in the vacant lot had predicted. The voice had also said that everything was going to be all right.

Carl thought about his dad doing drugs, hanging out with strange people, taking him to a Mob boss's house, gambling away money, telling lies, and fighting with his mom, and he wondered how everything could possibly be all right. Carl's family seemed to be spinning out of control.

And it all came to a climax one afternoon when a fight between his mom and dad turned deathly dangerous. Carl could hear his parents yelling at each other again, and for some reason he didn't try to hide this time. Instead he walked to the dining room and peeked through the open doorway into the kitchen.

"I've had it!" his mom yelled. "I won't live like this anymore!"

"What are you going to do about it?" his dad challenged.

Carl's mom snatched a butcher knife from the counter. Her jaw was clenched tight, and rage flashed in her eyes. His dad's face flushed with anger, and he picked up a knife as well. The two of them squared off in the kitchen. Carl had never seen his parents this out of control, and he knew that this time their fighting was different. Something inside told him that if he didn't do something fast, someone might die.

Carl didn't wait any longer. Boldly he stepped into the room.

"Stop!" he shouted at his parents. "I mean it! Stop!"

Carl bolted into the kitchen and wedged himself between the two knives, aware that the sharp blades were only inches from his face on either side. Carl felt adrenaline pumping through his veins as he waited, breathless. He looked up at each of his parents and knew he had to say what had been on his mind for a while now. He knew it would shock them, and he didn't know how they would react, so he took a deep breath before he spoke.

"Dad," Carl said slowly, "I want you to leave."

Both of Carl's parents looked at him, speechless.

Carl's mom spoke first. "Son, that's your father."

Carl nodded and talked fast. "I know, Mom. I know. But just listen. If you kill Dad, you'll go to jail, and Angel and I won't have anyone to live with. My uncles wouldn't even take care of us, because our family is involved with the Mafia."

Carl's mom slowly lowered her knife to the countertop; tears filled her eyes as she listened to him speak.

"And Dad," Carl continued, "if you kill Mom, you'll go to jail, and there will be no one to take care of us. What are we going to do then? You drink, you do drugs, you gamble, and you've endangered our family. I'm tired of all the lies, Dad. And I don't want you to be here anymore." Carl's voice faltered slightly. "I . . . I want you to leave, and don't ever come back."

When he was finished, he looked up into his dad's face, but he couldn't read his father's reaction. His father stood there speechless for a moment; then he threw the knife down on the floor and walked out the front door. Carl's mom started to cry.

It was hard to watch his father leave without even trying to salvage his family. Carl wished his dad would turn around and come back—that he would try to work things out and promise to stop his involvement with the Mob and his drinking and gambling, and be the father Carl and Angel needed. But he didn't.

He's choosing that life over us, Carl realized. It hurt, but he was convinced he had done the right thing by asking his father to leave. It was over.

Without his dad there to support them, the family's money situation changed drastically. Things Carl had taken for granted, such as a full refrigerator, new shoes, and extra money for the video arcade, were suddenly not in the budget.

With no other income options, Carl's mother took them down to the local welfare office and applied for food stamps. Carl felt humiliated as he stood in line with his mother to request help from the state. It was even more humiliating to go to the local grocery store and use a government handout to buy food to eat. Carl knew his mother didn't have a choice; she was only doing what she had to do for her family, but that didn't make it any easier.

"I always used to look down on poor people," Carl told Angel as they took groceries out of the brown paper bags and put them in the refrigerator.

"Me too," Angel said. "I just thought, *Why don't they just go get a job and make money?* Now we're the poor people."

"Yeah, now we know what this feels like. It doesn't feel good," Carl said.

"This is temporary," his mom promised the boys. "I don't like this any more than you do. I'm doing my best to find a job as quickly as I can."

His mom kept her promise. It wasn't long before she found a job working at a cafeteria, and they stopped receiving the government checks. She hardly made any money, though, and the little family had to get used to eating simple meals and living without all of the conveniences they were accustomed to having.

Fortunately for Carl and Angel, his father had seen fit to pay for their education at St. Jerome School in advance, so Carl was allowed to finish his final year at St. Jerome with his friends. Even though it had been his idea for his father to leave the family, he still terribly missed having a dad. No more afternoons bowling, no more dusty softball games, and no more pats on the back. There were also no more times for

Carl to spend with his dad learning about numbers or the code or the ins and outs of organized crime. Carl hadn't realized how much that time had bonded them together until it was gone. There was a big empty hole inside him where his relationship with his dad was supposed to be.

Life had definitely changed, and more changes were in store for Carl. After all the studying and preparation, his confirmation day finally arrived. Dressed in the nice clothes his mother had insisted he wear, he and his mom went down to St. Jerome School to attend the event. When they arrived, his mom sat down in the church, and he went in search of someone who could tell him where he was supposed to be for the service.

As Carl walked through the hallway behind the church platform, he heard noise coming from one of the rooms. Curious, he opened the door and looked inside. He recognized a couple of altar boys who were sitting in the room laughing. Carl realized that they had been drinking.

"Hey, what do you think you guys are doing?" Carl demanded when he saw the alcohol.

"Don't worry about it," one of the altar boys giggled. "It's cool. The priest gave it to us."

Carl was shocked to see one of the priests sitting in the corner. He was drunk too, and there were altar boys sitting with him. More was going on than Carl wanted to see. Feeling disgusted and angry, Carl closed the door and stumbled outside as fast as he could.

Looking back up at the church building where his solemn confirmation service was supposed to take place, he shouted, "God! How can You exist? These people are *Your* people?"

This was the final blow. But there was no answer from the tall brick building. No lightning. No voice from above.

"I can't trust my dad, I can't trust the priests, and I definitely can't trust You!" Carl continued. "So I guess . . . I guess I don't believe You exist."

Carl was furious, and as he stood there, he felt all of his anger and contempt harden into resolve. He was done with his dad, and he was done with God. He took one last look at the church building, and then walked away. And the empty place inside his heart grew larger.

CHAPTER 6

Carl was glad when his time at St. Jerome School was over. He was sick of hearing about God, he didn't want to see the priests he'd lost respect for, and he didn't feel like hanging out with his friends from school anymore.

Carl convinced himself he was an atheist. It was easier to pretend that God didn't exist than try to believe in the picture of God he had gotten at school. He decided that religion was for weak people, and he was anything but weak.

Forget Dad. Forget God. I'm better off taking care of myself. It's time for a new start, Carl decided.

His new start began one morning when the mail arrived. Carl thumbed through each piece quickly, looking for an envelope with his name on it. An advertisement, three bills, a sale paper, and then, what Carl had both dreaded and anticipated for days—an official-looking envelope addressed to him from Aviation High School.

"Please, please, please . . ." Carl said out loud, holding the letter to his chest.

Aviation High School was a public school in New York City that admitted only a small percentage of applicants from all over the city. Unlike a traditional high school that teaches general core subjects, Aviation High School prepared its students for a career in the aviation industry. Students who were admitted enrolled in rigorous technical classes that challenged their mathematic and scientific abilities. An additional program in Airframe and Powerplant certification from Aviation High School could help him earn up to four years of college credit by the time he graduated from high school.

Carl was pretty sure his grades and test scores were high enough for him to be selected, but the program was so competitive that he wasn't sure if he would make the cut. Now, with the envelope he had waited for in his hands, he could hardly bring himself to open it. Finally he tore it open and scanned the page for the news.

"Dear Carl, we would like to extend our congratulations . . ."

He had made it! Carl could hardly contain himself, and he couldn't wait for his mom to get home so he could share the good news with her. A tiny part of him wished he could share it with his dad, too, and see a look of pride on his father's face, but he shrugged away that thought. His dad's absence wasn't going to detract from his excitement. Not this time.

When his mother walked in from work, Carl showed her the letter. "Look, Mom, I got in!" he exclaimed.

"Carl, I'm so proud of you!" She hugged him tight. "I knew you could do it!"

For Carl, the rest of the summer dragged by. Though he would have normally played baseball and spent time with the neighborhood kids, this year Carl declined invitations from his friends and chose to be alone instead.

His friends were going off to other city high schools in the fall and were making choices Carl didn't agree with. He knew they were partying and having sex. Carl may not have had any religious values, but he was logical, and to him it didn't make sense to experiment with sex when there was risk of getting a girl pregnant or contracting a sexually transmitted disease. As far as the drugs and alcohol, he didn't see the point of starting to use the same substances that had torn his family apart. He had already seen what that kind of lifestyle could do to a person, and he wasn't impressed or even tempted when his friends invited him to party.

"No, thanks. I'm not into that kind of stuff," Carl told them.

"Are you a hard-core Christian now or something?" some of his friends teased.

Carl tried to control his temper. "No," he said, adding some swearwords to make his point. "I'm just not going to be stupid and throw my life away by getting addicted to drugs and alcohol or getting an STD."

That fall Carl began attending Aviation High School. He took his acceptance into the program seriously and studied hard. While most of his academic work centered on the technical aspects of aviation, he was excited to find out he also had classes on science and evolution. He was glad to finally explore an alternative to the theories of God and creation he had heard about at St. Jerome.

But the more Carl studied evolution and the big bang theory, the more questions he had for his teachers. He wanted to believe it, but he was never fully satisfied with their answers about how something could come from nothing.

It sounds like it takes faith to believe that everything was created by chance, and it also takes faith to believe in the idea that God created everything, he reasoned. *Either way, it takes faith.*

Carl began wondering if his decision to be an atheist might be wrong. It didn't take long, however, before a new idea came along that made him forget about his confusion between creation and evolution. It was an idea that was a portal to a dangerous world, bigger and more powerful than anything he had imagined. And he was about to enter in.

Carl walked into English class, slid into his desk, and opened his notebook. He preferred math. Or science. Or pretty much anything besides English. But when his English teacher got up from his desk and began talking, he started to think that this English class might be more interesting than any he had taken before. Carl sat up and listened.

"In each one of you is the power to become higher," his teacher said. "Each of you has the potential to evolve into a higher being. Each of us can become . . . well, become God if we want to. You can even develop energies that will help you read other people's thoughts."

For all his life Carl had been at the mercy of other people making decisions that affected his life. His father, his father's job, his mother's addictions—but now someone was telling him that he could take his life into his own hands and be in charge of his own destiny.

He raised his hand. "Can you explain what you mean? How does that work?"

The teacher looked at Carl and smiled. "Well, each of us has a spirit guide. If you listen, your spirit guide will whisper in your ear the things you need to know."

Carl was fascinated. He was about to ask another question when the teacher continued.

"Let's try it out now," his teacher said. "I want each of you to close your eyes and just try to imagine what I'm thinking."

Some of the kids giggled, but Carl closed his eyes and concentrated hard, imagining the energies his teacher was talking about and wondering about the idea of having a spirit guide. Suddenly a picture appeared in Carl's mind, and his eyes flew open. He raised his hand. Even before his teacher called on him, he knew without a doubt that somehow he had been able to read his teacher's mind.

"Yes, Carl?"

"You were thinking of a Boeing 747 commercial airliner flying across the sky from right to left," he said with certainty.

His teacher looked at him with a curious expression. "You're right," he said finally. "That's . . . very good."

This is cool, he thought. *I actually have these abilities!*

Instead of feeling like he was at the mercy of other people who might leave him or let him down, Carl actually felt powerful, special, and in charge of his own destiny.

On his way home he stopped at the library and thumbed through books about spirit guides and mind reading. He checked out a stack of volumes and took them home to study more closely. The more he read, the more fascinated he became with the dark, mysterious realm of spiritualism.

That night Carl drifted off to sleep with strangely compelling thoughts swirling in his head. Now that he was exploring the forces of spiritualism, he felt invincible—as if he could be anything he wanted to be and do anything he wanted to do. He was in charge. He wasn't going to answer to a Mob boss as his father did, or try to obey a confusing God. He had other plans for himself.

Before sunrise Carl woke up to the sound of his mother screaming. Confused, he opened his eyes and tried to get his bearings.

"What's going on?" he said, dazed.

"Wake up!" Carl's mom screamed, throwing his bedroom door open. "Cano! They shot him for payback! He's out there!"

"They shot Dad?" Carl was immediately awake, and his heart pounded hard as he and Angel tumbled out of bed and followed their mother downstairs.

CHAPTER 7

Carl's mother was crying hysterically, saying his dad's name over and over. "Cano, Cano, Cano!"

"Where is he, Mom? Where is he?" Carl demanded, taking her by the shoulders and trying to calm her down. "Talk to me!"

"He's out in the parking lot!" she cried. "He's lying out there on the ground! I saw him through the window!"

Carl and Angel bolted out the door and looked around in the early-morning darkness. Carl braced himself, afraid of what he would find.

"Do you see him?" Carl asked Angel.

"Over there!" his mom pointed from the porch.

Angel scanned the parking lot in the direction his mother pointed, and motioned toward a shadowed figure lying next to one of the cars. "There he is!"

Both boys raced across the parking lot in bare feet and knelt next to the still figure. When they rolled him over, Carl coughed at the strong smell of alcohol.

"Wait—this isn't Dad," Carl said, looking at the man's face. "And this guy hasn't been shot. He's just drunk."

Relief poured over Carl as he and Angel helped the man over to the curb before going back inside. He couldn't be upset with his mom for mistaking the figure on the ground for his dad. He knew that the possibility of his father's death caused fear to run deeply through all of them, especially with the news reports of Mafia-related shootings all over the city—even in restaurants and on street corners. Living with that kind of constant fear made the worst scenario seem inevitable.

"Mom, Mom, it's OK," Carl said, putting his arms around his mother. "It's not Dad. I'm sure he's fine. That was just a drunk guy on his way home from a bar or something. It wasn't Dad."

Carl fell back into bed, but he was too wired to sleep anymore. With the kind of activity his dad was involved with, and the rival Mafia families in the city, it was too easy to imagine his father paying the ultimate price for his choices. He tried to shake the thought from his head, but he couldn't help wondering where his dad was and wishing things could be different. For a moment he would have given almost anything to hear his dad snoring in the next room. But those days were over.

★★★

With God and Satan being ambiguous entities Carl didn't understand, a missing-in-action dad, and a mom who worked all the time, Carl liked the idea that he could be in charge of his own destiny and become whatever he wanted. Alone in his room, he began to study spiritualism and experiment with the energies his teacher talked about. Before long Carl was communicating with spirits, and he began to develop abilities that weren't normal, such as superhuman strength that enabled him to break a six-inch-thick board with his hand. He could also stop objects midair and hold them there with his mind.

When baseball season arrived the next spring, Carl tried out for a new team. The coach seemed impressed with his abilities, but there was something else that apparently made him even more interested in having Carl join the team. "You have the right aura," he told Carl.

"Aura? What is an aura?" he asked.

"A person's body is surrounded by an energy field that radiates colors of light. It's called an aura, and it can be an indication of someone's physical and mental health. Your aura tells me you're physically and mentally strong," his coach said.

Carl thought it was weird that he had been selected for a baseball team based on his "aura," but he was happy to be part of the team. As he got to know his new coach, he was fascinated to discover that his coach was very knowledgeable about some of the same spiritualistic practices he had been experimenting with. Carl continued to entrench himself deeper into the occult, and he soon grew to see his coach as a mentor not only on the baseball field but in his journey into spiritualism.

"Hey, Carl," his coach said one day after practice. "I'm having a meeting with some friends. I'd like you to come if you can make it."

"What kind of meeting?" he asked.

"You'll see," said the coach, smiling. "I think it's something you'll be very interested in. It has to do with some of the things we've been talking about."

That night Carl's baseball coach took him into a dark room with a number of other people. Lit candles lined the room, and as Carl and his coach sat down, the other people started chanting. "Repeat after us," some of the people instructed Carl. "We'll tell you what to say."

Feeling panicky, Carl looked around the strange room. He knew instinctively that something was very wrong, and he didn't feel safe. As he sat there, however, a bright white light appeared under the doorway, and a voice spoke to him, the same voice that had spoken to him in the vacant lot so long before. "Just keep your eyes on the bright white light, and you'll be OK," the voice said.

Carl concentrated on the white light under the doorway until the chanting stopped and someone turned the lights on. "You now have a spirit guide that will communicate with you," one of the people told him.

That night Carl lay in bed unable to sleep. He wished he had not gone to the meeting, and he wondered about the bright light and the voice. Had God spoken to him again? Was God protecting him from the strange, scary spiritual forces he had felt during the chanting session?

Suddenly a grotesque red face appeared above his bed. "You will serve *me*," the face said. It hovered above him on the bed, taunting him.

"No!" Carl tried to move and fight against this terrifying being, but his whole body was paralyzed. He knew the ugly red face wasn't God.

He tried to will himself into action, but no matter how hard he tried, he couldn't move. He was trapped.

CHAPTER 8

Terrified and unable to move, Carl closed his eyes and tried not to look at the demonic face hovering above him. He knew he had opened himself up to this experience by experimenting with the dark world of spiritualism. He had given demonic forces permission to be in his life, and now he was helpless to defend himself.

What do I do? I was so stupid to think I was in charge, he thought.

Carl suddenly remembered a picture his mom had put on the wall of Jesus praying in the Garden of Gethsemane. Carl had rejected God and pulled away from the idea He even existed, but now, as he lay in bed trapped under the dark spiritual forces he had opened himself to, Carl knew that if God did exist, He was the only one strong enough to fight the supernatural battle happening in his room. All of Carl's pride and self-reliance evaporated, and he choked out his own prayer: "God, if you exist, free me, and I will follow you!"

Immediately the red face disappeared through the wall, and Carl felt like he was falling through an elevator shaft. When the feeling left, he discovered he could move again. "Wow, God. You *do* exist," Carl breathed.

The next day Carl sorted through all of his books, pictures, and other items he had used in his spiritualist rituals and threw everything away. He couldn't wait to have it out of his room and out of his life—he was grateful he had the chance to start over, and he knew he would never be involved with any other spiritualistic rituals.

Carl was determined to keep his promise to follow God. The difficult part was that he still had all the same questions and confusion from before, and he had no idea how to start serving God.

"God," he prayed, "I want to follow You, but You've got to lead me. There are so many different churches. Where do You want me to be?"

That afternoon Carl decided to go to the library and begin studying the history of churches. *It's a start,* he figured.

As the days went on, Carl spent time reading everything he could find about church denominations and beliefs. During his studies he realized that Saturday was actually the Sabbath. *Why have we been going to church on Sunday for so long?* Carl wondered.

Based on his study, he decided to go to a Sabbathkeeping church. He continued to research the topic until he found a handful of denominations that celebrated Sabbath on Saturday. After attending two different Sabbathkeeping churches, he discovered that they held other beliefs that contradicted what he was learning about God. Dissatisfied, Carl kept looking.

One day one of Carl's friends invited him to join a baseball team. "It's my church's baseball team," Michael said, "and it's a Christian league, so you're going to have to behave yourself! But we really need your baseball skills."

"What church?" Carl asked.

"Seventh-day Adventist," Michael answered.

"We don't play any games on Saturday, though, because we keep the Sabbath."

Carl was immediately interested. It was then that he remembered attending a Seventh-day Adventist summer camp when he was younger, and he'd had a great time. "Sign me up!" he said.

Carl enjoyed his new baseball team. The kids were cool, and he loved what he was learning about the Bible from hanging out with them. But Carl had picked up some bad habits during his many years of playing baseball on non-Christian teams.

After a game one day, Michael took him aside. "Dude, you have to watch your language. This is a Christian league. We *want* you here, and I know you want to follow God, but following God also means you change the way you talk."

Carl tried to remember to keep his language clean, but it was a hard habit to break. Even though his heart was turned toward God, his mouth still wasn't, and he cursed a lot. With his bold and aggressive tactics on the ball field, his sportsmanship wasn't in line with his Christianity either.

One day during a game Carl's competitive spirit got the best of him. When one of his teammates made an error, he lost his temper and filled the air with swearing. He was still fuming during his next time at bat. He swung the bat hard, hit the ball and headed to first base, but the first baseman was in the way. Carl plowed over him like a bulldozer, hitting him so hard that he knocked him out.

This time one of the adults took him aside— a pretty cool guy named German.

"Carl," German said, "this is a Christian league. You can't behave this way, knocking people out and swearing."

"What do you want me to do?" Carl asked, still steaming.

German thought for a minute. "Well, let's see. Every time you're tempted to swear, say the words 'ice cream' instead."

Carl couldn't believe his ears. "Are you kidding me? I'll sound like an idiot. I'm not going to do that."

German smiled. "Try it."

The next time Carl felt the old vocabulary making its way out of his mouth, he quickly switched. "Ice cream!" Carl shouted. "Double ice-cream cone on you, with sprinkles on top!"

Carl's team members looked at him strangely, but German smiled and winked at him. Before long Carl stopped swearing altogether, and he didn't even need to say "ice cream" anymore.

Though his swearing days were behind him, he still had other habits to break.

Carl wasn't perfect, but he noticed his attitude was changing. He even started attending church every week. He actually loved what he was learning about God, and every time he attended a Bible study or worship service, he learned something new.

"Carl," one of the girls from church said one day, "do you own a Bible?"

"No," Carl admitted.

"Well, I brought one for you," she said. "Here."

Carl took the book in his hands and thumbed through the pages, intrigued by the idea that he could hold the Word of God in his hands. He was anxious to read it. "I don't really know where to start."

The girl smiled. "Why don't you start about halfway through in the book called Matthew? Those are the stories of Jesus. I think you'll like them."

When Carl got home, he started reading Matthew, then Mark, then Luke, and then John. What he read was a completely different picture of God than he'd had before. He read about Jesus healing people with the touch of His hand. He read about Him knocking over tables and chasing out of the Temple bad guys who were trying to cheat poor people. He read about the way the rulers and soldiers beat Him and put a crown of thorns on His head and nailed His hands and feet to a cross. Carl remembered that his dad had told him there was always a price to pay for choosing a better life, but as Carl read more and more about Jesus, he realized that Jesus had paid the price, and heaven was free to anyone who wanted to be there with God. That was a God Carl could understand and love.

"God," Carl prayed aloud, "I'm sorry for the way I've acted. The more I read about who You really are, the more I love You and admire You and want to be like You. I've always been aggressive and bold, but now I want to be aggressive and bold for You. Please help me."

Although Carl was making new friends at church, it was a little more difficult to make friends at school, so he spent a lot of time alone. Most of the guys at school had only one thing on their minds: girls. Carl liked girls too, but he didn't like the way the other guys talked about them and treated them. He wasn't impressed with the dirty stories the guys told or the tricks they used to make girls feel special so they could take advantage of them. Carl wanted to be like Jesus, and he couldn't imagine Jesus treating anyone so cheaply. Jesus valued people.

One day Carl overheard some guys talking. One of the guys was telling a story about how he had been able to convince a girl to get into the back seat of his car to have some "fun." His classmate was explaining every intimate detail of what had happened while they were there. The other guys were impressed; Carl was disgusted with the guy and embarrassed for the girl.

"I can't believe you're talking about it like this," Carl said. "That's not right. Show some respect."

"You gonna make me?" the guy laughed. "What, are you gay or something?"

Carl felt the old familiar adrenaline start to pulse through his veins. He knew it would take hardly any effort at all to knock the guy out and make his point. Instead, however, he took a deep breath and spoke. "I'm not gay. I just believe that girls should be treated respectfully, not like a toy that you use and throw away."

"Carl's gay!" some of the guys joked.

Carl turned and walked away. It wasn't worth it. They weren't the kind of guys he wanted to be friends with anyway, so he didn't really care what they thought of him. All around him people he knew were reaping the consequences of their decisions—from unwanted pregnancies to sexually transmitted disease to addictions—and he was trying desperately to make the right decisions.

It had been a long time since Carl had seen his father. German, the man from church who had helped him conquer his swearing habit, had become like a spiritual father to him, looking out for him and keeping him honest in his pursuit of God. Carl had also found a mentor in the church pastor. Both men took an interest in him, and when he would head down the wrong path, they would firmly guide him back to God. Carl realized that unlike the priests and his father, these men were honest and real, and he looked up to them. With the guidance of the two strong Christian men and his new understanding of God, things started to change in his life.

As he thought back to all the times he'd felt alone, he now realized that he had never been alone. God had been there all along, protecting him from his experimentation with demonic forces, sending angels to rescue him from a knife-wielding thief, and watching all of the baseball games his dad missed. The empty place in his heart was starting to heal thanks to God's intervention in his life and the guidance he was receiving from his mentors.

As Christmas approached and another year came to a close, Carl contemplated the many changes he had experienced in his life in the past few months. This year he had something to celebrate—the real reason for the season. As the snow fell around him, blanketing the lights and calming the buzz of activity in New York City, he thought about his choice to follow God and the peace he now had after turning away from a life of crime. When he sang about "peace on earth" at church, he knew he had made the right decision to trust God with his life. Someday he hoped he would have a wife and kids. As bold as he was in every other aspect of his life, he was a little shy when it came to girls, especially now that he had a God-shaped perspective. But he wanted a chance to do it the right way—a chance to base a home on God and love.

As he thought about his future and the prospect of his own family, his mind wandered to images of his dad. He just hoped that his dad could somehow find peace. "God, I know he's out there," Carl prayed. "I don't know where he is, but You do. You know my greatest fears for my dad. He can't keep doing what he's doing forever without paying the consequences. Please, God, find a way to save my dad."

CHAPTER 9

It wasn't long before Carl's pastor came to talk with him. "Carl," he said, "you've been with us for a while now, and you've made it clear that you want to follow God. I believe that it's time for you to be baptized."

Carl had seen baptisms before. Baptism is a symbolic action that publicly shows a person's decision to follow God. People who wanted to be baptized would go into a tank of water, and the pastor would tell the story of what made the person choose to follow God. Then the pastor would briefly dip them under the water as a symbol that their old life of sin and destructive decisions was over, and they were choosing a new kind of life with Jesus—washed clean, forgiven, and headed in a new direction.

He hesitated. "Uh . . . I don't know. I'll have to think about it." He remembered the other Sabbath-keeping churches he had attended that had other beliefs that conflicted with what he knew about God, and before he was baptized he wanted to make absolutely sure this was the church God had led him to.

Carl studied the Bible harder than ever, and he finally came to the pastor with a list of beliefs he had discovered in the Bible. When the pastor saw the list, he smiled. "Carl, those are all things we believe."

"Then I'm ready," he said. "Baptize me."

"There's one more thing," the pastor continued. "I have been impressed that you are being called to a ministry. I believe God is anointing you to work with youth and help kids to know Him."

It seemed like a strange calling at first, but the more he thought about it, the more he felt the Holy Spirit confirm what the pastor had said. He knew he was supposed to be doing for other kids what German and the pastor had done for him. Carl was baptized and immediately began working with kids in the church youth group and with a club called Pathfinders, which was a Christian version of Boy Scouts and Girl Scouts.

Before long, Carl had completed his coursework at Aviation High School. And as one of the top 50 students in his class, Carl was also able to go on to receive his Airframe and Powerplant certificate. The testing was rigorous, but Carl passed every exam. He was now qualified to work on any part of an airplane. The possibilities were beginning to open up for him.

"God, I'm not trying to be in charge of my own life anymore," he prayed one morning. "I want You to guide me and help me make the right choices about my future. I want to do what You have planned for me, not what I plan."

One of his options was to pursue more college education at DeVry, specializing in avionics. *Maybe I'll join the Air Force as an officer and learn to become a pilot*, he thought. His dad had been right about at least one thing: if a person works hard, eventually that hard work pays off, and Carl knew that a career in avionics could earn him a lot of money.

By the time he started at DeVry, Carl hadn't seen his dad in almost four years. But just when he was least expecting it, he received a visit from his dad, along with an unexpected and very expensive gift.

"For me?" Carl stood next to his dad and stared at the brand-new car in the driveway. It was a magnificent metal beast, with sleek lines, a shiny, perfect body, and a powerful, growling engine under the hood. In his wildest imagination Carl could not have come up with a more perfect car. He ached to get behind the wheel and test it out.

"Yes, for you," his dad answered, smiling. "Look, we've had our differences, but I want you to know I'm proud of you. You've worked hard, and you deserve a nice car. Go ahead! Get in!"

Carl felt a pain in his chest as he looked at the beautiful car.

"Well?" his dad said. "Are you going to get in it, or what?"

"Dad?" Carl said. "Can I ask you a question?"

"Of course," his dad answered.

"This new car you brought me," he said hesitantly. "I need to know. Is it from you? I mean . . . did you buy it with money you earned legally, or with blood money?"

Carl felt his father's attitude chill. "It doesn't matter," his dad said coldly. "A gift is a gift, Carl. You either take it or you don't."

Carl resisted the urge to accept the gift and avoid thinking about what his dad had done to earn the money to buy it. After a moment, though, his decision hardened to stone, and he spoke. "Dad, I love the car. It's beautiful. But if you bought it with Mafia money, I don't want it."

"You're turning it down?" his dad said through gritted teeth. "I give you a gift, and this is the way you treat me? You ungrateful—"

He snatched the car keys from Carl's hand and threw them at the new car with all his strength. Carl winced as the windshield cracked and splintered.

"I can't believe I came back for this," his dad seethed, and then he stormed away, leaving Carl standing there alone.

When Carl woke up the next morning and looked out the window, the car was gone. Turning down the car hurt, but his father's words and attitude hurt worse. He knew he had made the right decision. He could never have driven the car with a clear conscience, and he didn't want to feel guilty every time he sat behind the wheel.

Though it was hard to have his father abruptly out of his life again, Carl focused his attention on school and his new church friends. He felt his life slowly changing. Unlike a lot of his former friends, Carl wasn't interested in the dance scene or experimenting with drugs and sex. While he still had a "tough guy" attitude, he was also a gentleman—a combination that many of the church girls seemed to find attractive. Carl made friends with some of the girls from church, but kept his boundary lines firm.

Carl worked hard to earn good grades at DeVry. His mother didn't have money to pay for his schooling, and there were no scholarships available, so Carl got a job with Allied Aviation, a temp agency at John F. Kennedy Airport. They placed him in a job working for British Airways, and Carl was able to add valuable experience to the education he had received at Aviation High School. He worked grounds, which meant he dealt directly with the planes as they came and went—towing, fueling, loading and unloading luggage and supplies, as well as delivering mail to the international post office. In some ways Carl saw his job at the airport as a test.

Is this really what I want to do with my life? Carl wondered. *Work in aviation?*

Carl knew he would make a lot of money working in the aviation industry, but he knew that there was more to life than money, and most of all he wanted to do what God had planned for him. He knew that if he was doing what God wanted him to do, he would feel peaceful on the inside. On the flip side, if he wasn't doing what God had planned, his life would never feel right.

God, please just help me make the decisions I need to make, he prayed. *I have spent most of my life trying to be in charge of my own destiny. But now I'm turning it over to You. Just tell me where to go and what to do. In the meantime, help me be the person You need me to be wherever I am.*

It wasn't long before Carl discovered that most of the people he worked with didn't share his quest for honor and integrity. The fact that he was stubborn and vocal about what he believed didn't always make him popular with the other guys, either.

As Valentine's Day approached, Carl and his coworkers loaded and unloaded huge shipments of roses that were to be delivered to flower shops around the country. One day as they pulled boxes of roses from the cargo area, Carl noticed that a couple of guys had pulled a few dozen roses from the shipment and stashed them aside.

"What are those for?" Carl demanded. "What are you doing?"

"Keep your voice down!" one of the guys said. "We just pulled a few roses out for our girls for Valentine's Day."

"That's stealing," Carl said. "You need to put them back."

"We're not putting them back," the guy said. "What's your problem, anyway? There are hundreds of roses. They're not going to miss a few."

"It's wrong," Carl said. "Why would you take a chance like that, anyway? If you get caught stealing, you'll lose your job. Don't try to justify it."

The guys put the roses back, but they glared at Carl. "Watch out for Carl," they told the other workers. "He's a Christian, and he'll probably rat you out if he sees you doing anything he doesn't approve of."

"Carl, you'd never tell a lie, would you?" someone asked.

Carl shook his head. "Nope."

It was hard knowing that his coworkers were wary around him because he believed in doing the right thing. He wasn't trying to get anyone into trouble. In fact, he was trying to keep them out of trouble. Unfortunately the other guys didn't see it that way, and they purposely assigned him the most difficult tasks on the job. Carl didn't complain, even when the other guys took turns sitting in the warm mail truck while he worked out in the freezing temperatures. A few days later, however, Carl found himself in a sticky situation that tested his promise to tell the truth, as well as his relationship with his coworkers.

A new plane landed, and Carl and the guys scurried around doing their assigned jobs to stabilize the plane and handle the unloading and loading procedures. One of those procedures was to put in a pin that would keep the plane stable while the engines were shut off. It was a vital part of keeping the plane and the hundreds of pounds of cargo safe and stable until the engines were running again and the hydraulics could maintain the necessary pressure. This time a couple of the other guys were assigned to that task.

When the plane was loaded with passengers and cargo, Carl radioed the pilot to go over the checklist before takeoff. "Ground to pilot," Carl said over the radio. The engines were started, and he went down the list. When it was time, Carl reached to pull the pin out so the plane could be towed backward. Shocked, he realized the pin wasn't there at all. They had conducted the entire unloading and loading operation with the pin out!

"Pin release," the pilot said.

The pin is already out! Carl thought. *It was out the whole time!*

"Is the pin released?" the pilot prompted.

Carl hesitated. The other guys standing around him looked at him, knowing he had the power to get them into a lot of trouble if he told on them. Carl could see them imploring him with their eyes not to say anything about their mistake. It was a mistake that could cost them their jobs, and they were all waiting to see what he would do.

CHAPTER 10

"Pin release?" the pilot said again, sounding irritated.

Carl knew he had to make a quick decision about how to handle the situation. He took a deep breath. "My friends," Carl said, "the pin is out. Have a great flight."

The other guys were visibly relieved. One of them clamped him on the shoulder. "We love you, man," he said.

"Thank you for not getting us into trouble," the other guy said.

"And you kept us out of trouble without lying about it!" the first one said, shaking his head. "I guess it's possible to be yourself and still be one of us."

They gave Carl the rest of the day off, and when he came back to work, he was surprised to notice that they treated him as though he was part of the team instead of an outsider. It was as though they realized that Carl wasn't out to get them into trouble. He was just following his Christian beliefs, and they could respect that. They even started giving him assignments in the warm mail truck instead of out in the cold weather.

One day one of the guys Carl had confronted for stealing roses came to him privately. Though he had been angry with Carl for calling him out and stopping him from taking the roses at the time, now he had a kind of respect for Carl, and they had developed a good working relationship. "Carl, can I talk to you? I need your advice."

"Sure. What is it?"

"Well, this Christianity thing. It's real for you."

"Yeah?"

"I guess I just want to know how I could make it real for me," the guy said.

While they waited for the next plane to arrive, Carl sat with him on the conveyor belt and talked about God. He told him about his experience in discovering God in a real way, and he even took out his Bible to share some verses. The guy seemed really moved by what he was saying, and Carl sensed he was really ready to move forward and have a connection with God.

"Can I pray with you?" Carl asked.

The guy lowered his head a little, and then nodded. "Yeah," he said. "I need it."

Carl prayed with him right there at the airport amid the noise of planes taking off and landing. He realized that holding true to his beliefs had influenced this guy's decision for God. If he had never said anything about him stealing the roses, they wouldn't be here.

God, I don't know if this is the direction You want me to go with my life, but thank You for giving me the chance to be a positive presence in this guy's life, he prayed silently after they parted ways.

A few months later Carl attended a retreat with the youth from his church. It was a combined retreat with some other churches, and he met a lot of new people, including a girl named Mugett. They began to talk, and when Mugett found out he had a background in math, she had an idea.

"Why don't you talk with the principal at the academy—the local Christian high school?" she asked. "You could probably work as a tutor there. I know they would appreciate the help."

Carl shrugged, but he started thinking about it. He liked working with youth, and he loved math. Though Carl's job at the airport kept him busy, he was pretty sure he could fit in some time volunteering as a tutor for the students at the academy. He contacted the principal to talk about the tutoring opportunity, and before long, in addition to his studies at DeVry and his job at the airport, he was also tutoring students at the Christian high school.

"Mr. Rodriguez, you make it so easy," the students would tell him.

Parents also appreciated the way he tutored their kids, using real-life examples that made all the formulas and equations make sense. Carl felt good about his work at the academy, but again he felt a twinge of uncertainty.

God, this feels right, too, he said silently. He remembered what his pastor had told him when he baptized him, that he felt strongly that God was calling Carl to be involved with youth ministry. *Is this what I'm supposed to be doing?*

***

One day during his communications class at DeVry, Carl's teacher made an announcement. "During the past few weeks we've been talking about communication and public speaking," his teacher said. "Now, everybody knows engineers are known more for their mathematical abilities than their communications skills—"

Carl laughed along with his classmates. Most engineering students could solve complicated mathematical challenges, but because of the way their analytical minds worked, communication was a much more difficult feat than any complex engineering challenge.

"So," his teacher continued, "I've decided it's time to put what we've been learning about communication and public speaking to the test. You all knew this was coming. I'd like each of you to pick a topic you feel passionate about, because you're going to deliver an oral presentation to the class next week."

Most of the students groaned at the thought of talking in front of the class, but the wheels in Carl's mind started turning immediately. Something he was passionate about? That was easy—God. But this was a public institution, and most of the time the other students made fun of him when he mentioned anything about God or church.

Carl was still thinking about his presentation topic when class ended. As everyone gathered their notebooks and pencils to leave, Carl's teacher surprised him.

"Carl, I'd like you to stay after class for a moment, if you don't mind. I would like to talk with you about something."

Carl tapped his fingers on his desk as he waited for the other students to leave. He knew he hadn't done anything wrong, but he couldn't figure out why his teacher would want to talk with him. He sat at his desk and watched as his teacher took out a piece of bubble gum and popped it into his mouth. His teacher was trying to quit smoking, and whenever he wasn't lecturing, he would chew bubble gum to help curb his craving for a cigarette. When the classroom emptied, Carl walked up to his teacher's desk and swallowed. "You wanted to talk to me?"

His teacher sat back in his chair and looked up at him. "Yes," he said. "Look, Carl, I've noticed something about you. You're different than the other students."

"What do you mean?" he asked.

"Well," his teacher continued, still chewing his gum, "I never hear you curse. I never see you taking smoke breaks. You're just . . . different."

Carl understood exactly what his teacher was talking about then, and his face relaxed into a smile. "You're right—I am different," he said. "I don't swear. I don't drink. I don't smoke. It's because I'm a Christian."

"You're a good guy, Carl," his teacher said, picking up a stack of homework off his desk before he looked up again. "I just wanted you to know that."

"Thanks. Is that all you wanted to talk about?" he asked.

His teacher smiled. "Yes, that's all I wanted to tell you. Thanks for sticking around."

Carl picked up his backpack and started to walk out of the room, but he paused at the door. "Can I ask you something? I have an idea for the public speaking presentation that's coming up, but I want to get your permission for my topic."

"What's the topic?"

"If it's OK with you, I would like to talk about creation versus evolution—purely from a philosophical and scientific viewpoint."

Carl's teacher paused and looked down at the desk. "Well, we've never done anything like that before." He chewed his gum thoughtfully for a moment, and then nodded. "You know what? Go ahead. You'll have 30 minutes to present your case, and then the other students will have an opportunity to ask you questions. This will be interesting. Good luck."

All week, as Carl tutored his students and worked at the airport, he prayed that God would give him the right words to say and that he would present his topic in a way that would help people become more interested in God. When the day of his oral presentation arrived and Carl stood up to speak, he wasn't nervous at all.

"Most of you already know that I'm a Christian," Carl began. "And since the assignment was to talk about something I'm passionate about, I've chosen to talk about creation versus evolution. There are a lot of reasons I've chosen Christianity as my path. But today I want to talk to you purely from a scientific and philosophical viewpoint."

The class was quiet while Carl spoke. "If you've chosen to subscribe to the theory of evolution, you've adopted the premise that everything just happened by chance. That one day a big bang ignited the potential for life, and everything evolved from that. You even have a formula that says that a wormhole shrunk, then exploded. But I have a question for you."

He looked around the room at his classmates. "The data tells us that energy or matter existed before the big bang. Where did the energy or matter come from to create that big bang? It had to have come from somewhere. Scientists believe that it just existed. Let me tell you what it takes to believe that. It takes faith. You know what the definition of religion is? It's having faith in something you can't prove. Therefore, a belief in evolution, since it requires faith, is a religious belief."

The teacher and the other students listened intently while he spoke. Even James, the long-haired, glossy-eyed hippie who always smelled like marijuana, was leaning forward.

"If I assume that evolution is correct, and I believe it's all about survival of the fittest, then life is only about me and living for the moment. Because if I die, I just go back to substance and energy, and nothing matters anymore."

He paused and let the words sink in. He was surprised that even students who had made fun of his religious beliefs were paying attention to what he was saying.

"Now let's talk about the creation side of things. I'm not going to try to prove creation. All I want to do is ask you to imagine with me. Imagine that an alien being did supply the energy or matter that started the evolutionary process. Or take it a step further and imagine that there was a deliberate Designer who created us on earth. If on any level our existence was planned or designed, then there is a purpose for us. Here's the difference. If I was created with a purpose, then I can live outside of myself. I can live for other people. I can live for God."

Carl walked around the desk and picked up a piece of chalk. He drew a line down the center of the chalkboard and began to write. "Let's back up and look at the two things. If you believe in evolution and you live only for yourself in survival-of-the-fittest mode, and you die, that's it. If you believe in creation and you die, you have something more than this life to look forward to. If you live with purpose—if you live morally, take care of your body, and serve other people—is there anything wrong with that? You're more at peace and you treat people differently—the way I treat you as my classmates. And after you die and Jesus comes again, you go to heaven to be with God."

When he was done writing on the board, he took a step back so his classmates could see what he had written. Under creation he had written: "End results: happier life and live with God." Under evolution he had written: "End results: selfish life and absence from God." He turned around and looked at the class. "I'm not trying to make you into a Christian. I'm just trying to make you think. If you look at one versus the other, what option is most in your favor?"

He finished his presentation, and his classmates clapped. Then James the hippie raised his hand.

"Yes?" Carl said, pointing to James.

"Man, this is deep, man. Deep. Man, you really believe this, right, man?" James said.

"Yeah, I really believe this," Carl said. "What do you think?"

James seemed as though he was trying to collect his thoughts. "I think I've noticed you, man. You're different. You're different to people."

No longer talking from his notes, Carl looked at James. "You know why? I feel like I've tasted who God is. Before I met God, I was sour. It was all about me, and I lived in fear. Now everything's different. With God in my life I can treat other people differently. I'm not afraid of dying. I don't have to always be looking out for number one. That's why I can treat you the way I do."

When class was over, Carl wasn't sure if anything he had said really had an impact on anyone. Nobody said much to him as they left class, so he gathered his things and left. The next day, however, something had changed.

"Do we have a new student?" Carl's teacher asked, looking at the back row.

Carl turned around to look and couldn't believe his eyes. It was James. At least it looked kind of like James, except he had shaved his beard and gotten a haircut, he was wearing clean clothes, and his eyes were clear and unclouded by drugs.

"James? Is that you?" Carl couldn't stop staring.

"Yeah, man," James said. "For some reason, when you were talking yesterday . . . well, I can't explain it, but I was hanging on every word, man. What you said—I got it. I gave my life to God, man. This is incredible, man. This is incredible. Thank you!"

Carl could barely contain himself. *God,* he prayed. *Here I am in a non-Christian school with non-Christian people. I was allowed to give a presentation about*

You, and a kid turned his life over to You. The way You work is unbelievable."

When class ended, Carl's teacher caught him before he left. "Carl, don't take this wrong, but you don't belong here. I'm not religious or anything, but I think you're supposed to be a pastor. You're bright, you get good grades, but after hearing what you said yesterday . . . well, you're supposed to be a pastor."

Is God using my non-Christian professor to help me figure out what my life path should be? Carl wondered. *What do I do now?*

Though Carl's public speaking had impressed his communications professor, his academic performance impressed some of the other faculty, and it wasn't long before a representative from an engineering laboratory approached him with an offer he couldn't pass up, and his thoughts of being a pastor faded to the background.

"Carl, this is an important offer," the representative told him. "We would like to offer you a position working at the laboratory this summer. We'll pay you for your time. In addition, we will pay for your schooling. Also, if you would like a permanent position at the lab after your initial summer, there will be a job waiting for you. We have very few Blacks and Hispanics in our program, and we'd like you to join us. We see great potential in you."

Carl leaned forward in his chair and looked at the representative. "Are you telling me," Carl said slowly, "that you're going to let me work for you for one summer, then you're going to pay for my schooling so I don't have to work, and then when I graduate, you'll give me a job?" It sounded too good to be true.

"Yes, that's what I'm saying," the representative said.

"That's a no-brainer," Carl said. "Of course I'll come work for you. On one condition," he added.

"What's that?"

"I want to make sure you're not offering me this position just because I'm Hispanic and you need a certain number of Hispanic recruits. I work hard, I get good grades, and I'm not interested in charity just because of my race."

The representative smiled. "Carl, I assure you this offer is because of your grades and how hard you've worked. We like what we see in you."

Carl was excited about his new position at the lab and looked forward to pouring himself into his work. *This must be an answer to prayer,* he thought. *And if it is, I don't care what field God places me in; I'm going to give it my best.*

What he didn't know was that he was about to embark on one of the worst experiences of his life.

CHAPTER II

"D on't tell me you actually believe in that stuff," said Ben, one of Carl's fellow lab workers, as he thumped on Carl's Bible and laughed. "Look, everybody, Carl still believes in fairy tales! Do you believe in Santa and the Easter Bunny, too?"

Carl sighed and tried to concentrate on his work. It was bad enough that he was swamped with difficult work, but to have his fellow workers making fun of him all the time for his Christian beliefs was really getting old. Most of the people he worked with came from prestigious schools and had wealthy families, and they felt they were too smart to believe in God.

God, did You put me here to show me where I shouldn't be? Carl griped silently. *I'm sick of this. Nobody here cares anything about You, and all they do is make fun of me. What am I doing here?* The old Carl would have gotten in their faces. Christian Carl bit his tongue and tried to let his work and his positive attitude be the example.

"Carl!"

Carl looked up from his desk to see his supervisor walking in his direction.

"Yes?" he answered.

"I have a project for you," his supervisor said, dropping a thick stack of papers in front of him. "I'm not going to lie—this is a tough one. It'll probably consume you for about six weeks if you are on top of it. But I think you can handle it."

When Carl examined the project, he felt overwhelmed. It was a massive, difficult assignment. The supervisor was right—this project could swallow him whole.

OK, God, Carl prayed again. *You put me here. I can't figure out why, but I'm here. You're the one who gave me these skills in the first place, and You are the author of creativity. I need You. Anybody can have wisdom that comes from textbooks, but I need the wisdom that comes from You. Please give me Your wisdom and Your Spirit.*

Before he started on the project, Carl picked up his Bible. Ignoring the jokes from his fellow workers, he read the book of Ecclesiastes and soaked in the words about wisdom. Then he went to work.

As he immersed himself in the project, he found that, surprisingly, it all made sense. Complex calculations and solutions seemed to come out of nowhere as he worked to finish the assignment. To his own amazement, he finished in only a few days.

When he walked into his supervisor's office with the completed project, his supervisor stared at him in apparent disbelief. "You're *done?* Are you *kidding me?*"

"It's all there," Carl said. "Finished."

"Carl, can you show me how you did this?" his supervisor asked, thumbing through his work with an amazed look on his face.

Carl nodded.

"Wait." His supervisor got up from his chair and walked to the office door. "Everybody, stop what you're doing and come in here. Carl just finished a six-week project in a few days. I've asked him to show me how he did it, and I think it would be beneficial if everyone listened in."

Carl's fellow lab workers assembled in the office to hear Carl's explanation.

"First, I want to start by saying congratulations to Carl," his supervisor said when everyone filed into the room. "Because you've turned this project around so quickly, I'm going to reward you. This incredible completion just earned you a one-week paid vacation."

"Wow. Thank you," Carl said while everyone clapped. "Can I take it starting today?"

"Yes! You can leave now, if you want—but first, tell us how you did it." The supervisor and all of the other lab employees looked at Carl expectantly.

"Well," Carl said. "See that book over there?" He pointed to his Bible. "That's my only secret. Anybody can obtain knowledge, but wisdom comes from God. God is the one who gave me the wisdom to complete the project so quickly."

Carl's supervisor looked at him in stunned silence, while the other employees started laughing. "*God* did your project for you?" someone called out, and then others joined in with the jokes.

"Laugh all you want," Carl said to his peers. "But that's how the project got finished." Carl's face burned a little, but he stood tall and looked his supervisor in the eye. "With all due respect, sir, can I leave now?"

The supervisor nodded yes, and Carl turned and walked out of the office. He couldn't believe he had an entire week off work—paid!

"What am I going to do for a whole week?" Carl

said as he walked into his house and put his keys on the counter. Just then the phone rang. It was German.

"Carl, I know this is last-minute, and you probably can't get the time off work, but I have to ask. I have a campout with the Pathfinders starting tomorrow. I need some help with the boys. Is there *any* way you could come along and assist me with the kids?"

Carl laughed. "You're not going to believe this, German, but . . ." He explained about the week of paid vacation.

"You've got to be kidding!" German laughed. "Well, get your sleeping bag and your marshmallows ready! We're going camping!"

Carl had a great time working with the Pathfinder kids, and again he started wondering about his career choice. Though he was good at it and was making a lot of money, his job as an aviation engineer at the lab was miserable.

Maybe I'm supposed to be working with kids instead! Carl thought. There was something rewarding about mentoring kids the way that German had mentored him when he had first started coming to church.

★★★

Summertime in New York City was hot and sticky, and with school and work Carl hardly had time to think about anything else. That is, until one afternoon when he stopped at a gas station mini-mart for a cold drink. As he walked through the doors the headline from the New York *Daily News* caught his eye, and he stopped. He picked up the newspaper, which read: "'GODFATHER' GALANTE SLAIN—Mob Chief & Two Others Die; 4th Is Shot in B'klyn Rubout."

Carl could hardly look at the picture on the front of the paper without feeling sick. Two blood-soaked bodies, Mob boss Carmine Galante and his associate Nino Coppolla, were sprawled across the ground in the backyard dining area of Joe and Mary's Restaurant in Brooklyn. Galante still had a cigar smoldering in his mouth. The restaurant owner and his son were also shot, but four anonymous hooded men had escaped in a car after the rubout. "Retirement, Mob-style," the caption read.

Looking at the photo and reading the story, Carl knew he was getting an inside peek at the world his father had chosen to be part of, and he couldn't shake the feeling that if he had not asked his father to leave, he might be part of that world now too. He remembered the gun he had found under the front seat of his father's car when he was younger, and he wondered how many horrific newspaper headlines his father's gun had caused.

God, I know my father is not a good man, Carl silently prayed as he put the newspaper back on the rack, *but please . . . don't let him die that way. He can't rescue himself from the life he chose. I don't think he could find his own way out even if he wanted to now. If he's going to be saved, You're going to have to be the one to rescue him.*

Summer faded into long, hot afternoons and cooler evening breezes that whispered of fall. As Carl drove through the busy streets full of kids enjoying their final days of vacation before school began, something was bothering him. He had something in common with his father—he liked to make money. If he stayed with his job at the lab, he would make plenty of money as an aviation engineer. He would easily be able to provide well for a family someday. But if he went in the direction of ministry, money would not exactly be one of the benefits. He knew that pastors and ministry workers barely eked out a living in most cases. Was he ready to trust God with something as basic as knowing where his next paycheck was coming from?

I trust You with everything else, he told God. *I guess I can trust You with that, too.*

As he closed the door to the car and walked into the house, something strange happened. A moving picture appeared in front of him, and he was in it. He was standing in front of a classroom teaching math to some students.

"I want you to be a teacher for two years," a voice said.

"What?" Carl said out loud, watching the scene play out in front of him. "This is crazy!"

"I want you to be a teacher for two years," the voice said again, more insistently.

Carl blinked, and the picture suddenly disappeared. He was still in his living room, standing there as if nothing had happened.

"What in the world was that about?" he asked the voice. "God? Was that You?"

A few minutes passed, and Carl was still a little shaken up. He knew that the vision he had seen was real—just as plain as if he were watching a movie of himself. He went through every detail of the vision over and over in his mind.

Just then the phone rang, and Carl couldn't believe who was on the other end of the line.

CHAPTER 12

Carl answered the phone.

"Carl, this is David Cadavero," the voice on the line said. David Cadavero was the principal at the academy where Carl had been tutoring.

"Yes, what can I do for you?" Carl asked.

"I can't give you all the details," David said, "but we lost a teacher. We need you to teach at our school. In fact, we want you to be the chair of the math department."

Carl was stunned. He could feel tears forming in his eyes. "I'm going to have to call you back," he said. He hung up just before he broke down crying.

That was *You!* he said to God. The vision was real. The call confirmed it. After a few minutes he was able to stop the flood of tears, wash his face, and call David back.

"Sorry I hung up on you like that," Carl said. "Boy, do I have a story to tell you later. I'm totally overwhelmed, but I will definitely take the job."

"Great!" David said.

"There are just a few things I have to handle first," Carl said. "It's August, and I'm supposed to be in school at DeVry until October. I'm going to have to go talk to my teachers."

"Do whatever you need to do," David said.

Explaining to his teachers why he wanted to stop coming to class three months before he was scheduled to graduate wasn't an easy task.

Most of his teachers had the same response. "Carl, you have spent all this time and money on college. You're working at the lab. You have a good job waiting for you as soon as you graduate. You're going to throw all of this away?"

"I'll tell you what," Carl said. "If you'll give me a waiver, I'll come back and take the final even though I can't come to class for the last three months."

Each of the teachers reluctantly agreed, and Carl was able to start his teaching job the next day. The representative from the laboratory where Carl worked didn't take the news quite as well. In October when Carl went back to DeVry to take his final examinations, the people from the laboratory wanted him back. They didn't like the fact that he had changed careers.

"Carl, we're prepared to make you a really good offer," the representative prodded, but Carl wouldn't budge.

"Look, don't take it personally, but God asked me to teach young people for two years. And when He asks, I follow."

Even so, with all of his teachers and his potential employers at the lab looking at him like he was out of his mind for leaving behind all of his opportunities in order to teach at a Christian school, Carl began to have his doubts.

Am I really doing the right thing? he wondered. The vision he had seen in his house seemed like a long time ago, and his courage wavered as he thought of everything he was giving up.

Just after final exams his classmates invited him to a party to celebrate.

"What kind of party will it be?" Carl asked. "A party to celebrate our accomplishment, or an excuse to drink alcohol and smoke weed and hang out with girls?"

"Carl, you're such a party pooper," his classmates said. "You are never up for having a good time."

"If that's what you call having a good time," he said, "then you'll have to do it without me."

A few days later Carl stopped by the school to pick up his papers. While he was there he saw some of his classmates, and one of them called him aside.

"Carl, you put us to shame," he said.

"What do you mean?" Carl asked.

"I know you don't know this," the kid said, "but I'm a Christian."

"You are?" Carl was surprised. "I've attended school with you for this long, and I never knew. You never said anything."

"Yeah, I know. I didn't want to show it, because . . . well, I wanted to be popular and fit in. I let you think you were the only one, but really, there are a few of us here. We should have stood up with you about the party and made it a celebration instead of an excuse to drink and do drugs. But, we let you down because we made you stand for what was right all by yourself. I'm sorry."

"Well, I forgive you," Carl said. "I'm not about putting people down or making them feel bad. You know that."

"I know. Thank you," the kid said. "One more thing. We all know that you're leaving to go teach at a Christian school. I just want you to know—we all think you're doing the right thing."

Carl felt warm inside. All of his doubts about leaving to go teach at the academy were erased, and for once in his life he knew he was doing exactly what God wanted him to do.

Graduating and becoming chair of the math department at the academy at such a young age were huge accomplishments for Carl, but being just barely older than his students sometimes made things interesting at the school. Some of the older girls would flirt with him and ask him out. Even though he was their age, Carl knew that as their teacher he had to draw strict boundary lines, and he refused to date any of his students.

During parent/teacher conferences, parents would walk into his office and ask for Mr. Rodriguez. Carl had fun saying, "Yes, that's me—I'm sitting right here," and watching their jaws drop when they discovered that a "kid" was actually chair of the math department.

The next couple of years went by quickly, and Carl vaguely remembered that God had asked him to teach for only two years. When Carl began teaching his final semester at the academy, he wondered what God had planned for him. He could hardly wait to see where God would lead him next.

★★★

Carl noticed her right away—a new girl on campus. He knew all the students, and he had never seen her before, so he knew she must be a new addition to the student body. He had heard other teachers call her

Mary, but since he hadn't met her yet, he walked up to her and put his hand out in a friendly gesture.

"Welcome to the academy," Carl said. "Your name is Mary, right?"

She looked at his hand, then back up at him before she shook her head and walked away. "Nice try," she said, flinging her hair over her shoulder.

Carl felt his face grow warm. *She thinks I'm a student trying to hit on her,* he thought. *She is very pretty, and we are close in age. If the situation were different . . .* He stopped and shook his head. *She's a student, and you're a teacher,* he reminded himself—his boundary lines had to stay very clear in his mind.

"She's a new transfer," one of the other teachers told him later. "Her name is Mary Espejo. She's not a Christian, but her grandmother is. She wasn't doing well in public school, and wanted to try coming here. We all need to do our best to make sure she feels welcome."

When Mary found out Carl was actually a teacher, she apologized. "I'm sorry!" she said. "I didn't realize . . . I just thought you were being rude!"

Carl laughed. "Apology accepted. I wasn't trying to be rude; I was trying to be friendly! So why did you decide to transfer in the middle of the school year?"

"Honestly," Mary said, "I just hated public school. The focus is so different from what I want. I want to change my life around—you know, start doing things right. And it's so hard in an atmosphere like that. That's why I wanted to come here."

"Well," Carl said, "why don't you come to church on the weekend? I'll introduce you to the youth leader. It will be a great place for you to make some new friends and get that fresh start you're looking for."

Mary agreed and started attending church. Since Carl was involved with the youth activities, he invited Mary to go on all the outings, and it wasn't long before she made friends at the church and attended all the activities.

School ended, and so did Carl's job at the academy. Summer found Carl unemployed, without a clear direction, and running out of money.

OK, God, Carl often prayed. *Anytime You want to tell me what to do next, I'm listening. If You want, I could go back to engineering. I wouldn't mind fattening up my bank account after two years of teaching!*

It wasn't long before God answered in the same voice Carl had become accustomed to hearing. "Carl, I want you to go to college and take theology. You're going to be a youth pastor."

Youth pastor, huh? Carl said. *I have no money. Do you expect me to show up at a university with no money and no job and tell them I want to go to school? They're going to laugh at me.*

Carl had heard about the theology program at Atlantic Union College, and as he researched the program, he felt impressed that God wanted him to go to school there. Summer was almost over, and time was running out.

OK, Lord, I'll make a deal with You. I'll drive to Atlantic Union College and ask them to accept me with $5. If this is really Your will, they'll take me with $5, and I'll find a job to pay for my schooling. If they *laugh at me, I'll take that as Your answer to go back to engineering.*

Carl summoned his courage to drive three and a half hours by himself to Atlantic Union College, praying the whole way. When he arrived, he stared at the long sidewalks and the pillars lining the brick buildings. Could he really attend school with only $5 in his pocket?

Carl walked to the registrar's office and told the woman at the desk that he wanted to apply to be a student. She asked him several questions about what field he was interested in, what his experience was, and where he was from.

"How do you plan to pay for your schooling?" the woman finally asked.

"Well, that's the thing," he said. "I need you to accept me into your program with $5. That's what I have."

The woman looked up at him as though she was trying to figure out if he was serious or not. When she saw his face, she realized he wasn't kidding.

"Look," she said, "I can get your application going for you, but you're going to have to come up with more than $5. We can't accept you as a student with a $5 deposit."

So that was it. Carl thanked her, and then turned to walk down the hallway. God had given him an answer, and the answer was no. It seemed strange that God would send him all this way only to have his request turned down, and now all he had to look forward to was a three-and-a-half-hour drive home.

"Hey! You—in the blue shirt! Stop!"

Carl turned around and saw a man motioning to him.

"You mean me?" he asked.

"Yes, you," the man said. "I overheard your conversation with the registrar. I need to talk to you."

"What is it?" Carl asked, walking toward the man.

The man looked at him closely. "There's more to your story, right? More than what you told her?"

"Well, yes," he began. "Why do you ask?"

"God just told me you need to be a student here. I want you to go ahead and sign up to be a student today."

Carl's jaw dropped. "What . . . ?"

The man smiled and put his hand on Carl's shoulder. "Are you OK?"

"Yes," Carl nodded. "I just didn't expect . . . I thought the answer was no."

The man told Carl how to obtain his transcripts and when classes would start. A little while later Carl left Atlantic Union College as a registered student with a tuition payment of only $5.

CHAPTER 13

S o that's how I became a student," Carl told his family after he recounted the entire story to them.

He could see that his mother was proud of him, and his aunt Karen couldn't stop smiling. "You've come a long way, Carl. There was a time we were worried that you would follow in your father's footsteps."

Carl looked up at the mention of his father. "Have you seen or heard from my dad at all?"

"I saw him a while back," Aunt Karen said. "Wait until I tell you what happened. But you can't tell anyone at all, not my daughter Elena, or anyone."

"OK," he agreed. "What happened?"

"Well, we found out that Elena was going to have a baby. It was a huge surprise for all of us. She had been dating this boy for a while, but they weren't married. When it came to taking responsibility for his actions, her boyfriend stopped coming around. We thought he was going to leave her to raise a baby all by herself."

"Oh, no," Carl said. That was one of the reasons he had chosen not to get physical with girls the way his friends did. That kind of involvement had the potential to affect a lot of people's lives, and he wanted to wait until he was married and ready for the responsibility of a family. "What happened?" he asked.

"Well, your dad found out about it," Aunt Karen said. "He handled it Mafia-style. He showed up at the home of the boy's father with a gun and told him it was very simple. Either he could be at the church for his son's wedding to Elena, or he could be at the church for his son's funeral."

"What?" Carl was amazed but not necessarily surprised that his father would make threats like that. After all, that's what he did for a living.

"He told the boy's father that if his son left within two years, he would find him, and there would be a funeral." Aunt Karen took a sip of tea and looked at Carl. "Your dad . . . you can't mess with him. The boy was so afraid he showed up at the wedding and married Elena. They stayed together only a year. Elena told everyone she threw him out, but that might have just been to save him from your dad."

Carl shook his head. "I wonder where he is now."

Aunt Karen took his hand. "I don't know. But there's a reason I told you that story," she said. "I want to affirm you in your decision to be a pastor. You're going to have an effect on people's lives also, just like your father. But it's going to be different than your father's way. You made the right choice."

With his aunt Karen's affirmation in mind, Carl began to prepare to attend Atlantic Union College in the fall. Massachusetts was a long way from the home he knew in New York, but Carl looked forward to living away from the big city.

There was only one thing that made leaving difficult. He had been spending a lot of time with Mary, and had gotten used to her beautiful smile and her company. Carl had invited her to every summer outing, and she had attended them all, but he had been very carefully guarded in his friendship with her.

A few days before Carl left for Atlantic Union College, Mary took him aside. "Carl," she said, "this whole summer you've been inviting me to go to different events."

"Yes," he said. "What are you trying to say?"

"I want to know something. Are we going to continue to be just friends?" Mary looked up at him with her pretty eyes. "You're not my teacher anymore. Are you ever going to ask me out, or are you too shy?"

Carl suddenly did feel very shy, and his heart started beating faster. "Can I get back to you on that?" he asked softly.

Mary laughed. "Yes . . . well, I just thought I'd put that out there."

Carl couldn't stop thinking about it. Did it make sense to ask her out when he was getting ready to leave and be away at school? He knew he liked her, but he wasn't sure it was a good idea to take the next step and be more than friends. Finally he decided just to talk to her about it.

"Mary," Carl said when he saw her the next day, "I'm leaving. I'm going away to college. It's not going to be easy, but I want to stay in touch with you. That is, if you're willing to explore this long-distance."

Mary promised to write, and she did. Far away, at Atlantic Union College, Carl began looking forward to each envelope with Mary's handwriting on it. He wrote back often during the next year, telling her all about his life and schooling there. When he read her letters, he could almost hear her voice and see her facial expressions, and when she opened up about what she was learning about God and the direction her life was taking her, he was touched by what a wonderful person she was. He surprised himself when he finally realized he could fall in love with this girl.

God, what should I do? he prayed. *Please help me. If this is right, I want to move forward in our relationship. If it's not, then I don't want to string her along and break her heart . . . or mine.*

One day, while Carl was praying, he felt a strong impression to read Isaiah 62:4, 5. He opened his Bible and read: "No longer will they call you Deserted, or name your land Desolate. But you will be called Hephzibah, and your land Beulah; for the Lord will take delight in you, and your land will be married. As a young man marries a maiden, so will your sons marry you; as a bridegroom rejoices over his bride, so will your God rejoice over you." The next time he prayed, he again felt a strong impression to read Isaiah 62:4, 5. Every time he prayed and asked God whether or not he should move forward in his relationship with Mary, he was impressed to read it again, until he finally decided to memorize the verses.

Carl couldn't wait until he had a break from school and could go back to New York to see Mary. The three-and-a-half-hour drive seemed to take forever, but he knew every minute was worth it when he saw her come running out the front door to greet him. After they had said hello, Carl motioned for her to sit down next to him on the front porch.

"Mary, I need to ask you something. The Lord has impressed me to read this text. He won't leave me alone about it, and I've read it over and over. I even memorized it, finally," Carl said. "It's Isaiah 62:4, 5. Does that mean anything to you?"

Mary looked away for a moment, and when she looked back, she had tears in her eyes that threatened to spill down her cheeks.

"Mary, are you all right? What's wrong?" Carl asked, looking down at her.

"I'm all right," she said, laughing even while she cried. "It's just that . . . I've been praying to God about us . . . about what we should do. I prayed that if it is God's will for us to get married, He would give you that text. And He did."

Carl felt his own eyes getting teary, but he was too excited to care. "Then let me go get permission from your grandmother to officially start courting. I want to marry you, Mary."

Mary looked up at him and smiled, her lashes wet with tears. "I want to marry you, too."

Carl hesitated. "Mary, there's only one thing that would hold me back from marrying you. I won't marry someone who hasn't chosen to be a Christian. I want to make sure that's what you want, because that's what my life is about."

"I'm already planning to be baptized soon, Carl," Mary assured him.

"Don't do it for me," he said.

Mary laughed. "I'm not. I'm getting baptized for me. My relationship with God has been unfolding for a long time now. You just happen to be a good catch!"

Two days before Valentine's Day, Carl and Mary

said their vows and became husband and wife, with their family and friends there to celebrate with them. With her recent baptism and marriage to Carl, Mary decided she wanted to make another symbolic move to represent her new life with God and Carl. When she changed her last name to Rodriguez, she also changed her first name to Maria.

Carl and Maria moved to Massachusetts so Carl could finish his schooling at Atlantic Union College, and a little more than two years later Carl and Maria welcomed a little baby girl into their home. They named her Elizabeth.

Carl was excited to be a dad. As he looked into Elizabeth's tiny face, he knew that he would do everything he needed to do to protect her and be a good father to her. Most of all, he wanted to give her something his father had never given him. *My father raised me in the shadow of the Mob,* he thought. *I'm going to raise my daughter in the shadow of the cross.*

CHAPTER 14

When springtime arrived, Carl and Maria and little Elizabeth traveled to New York to visit their family. As often happened when he returned to the city, Carl's thoughts turned to his father. *Is he OK? Where is he?*

Carl asked around until he figured out where his father was staying. With Maria by his side and Elizabeth in his arms, Carl knocked on the front door. There was no answer. Carl knocked again, and this time he heard someone shuffling around on the other side of the door. He knew his father was aware they were standing on his doorstep.

"Dad!" Carl called. "Dad, you can shut me out. But don't shut out your little granddaughter. I want you to meet Elizabeth."

The door opened a crack, and Carl could see a sliver of his father's face. When his father looked down and saw Elizabeth, he swung the door open wider and motioned them inside.

Carl unwrapped Elizabeth and placed her in his father's arms. "This is your grandpa," Carl whispered to Elizabeth. He could see the pride on his father's face as he held his little granddaughter.

"Dad, you know I love you," Carl said. "But I worry about you. I don't approve of what you're doing. You know what you're doing is wrong and dangerous. I want you to be able to be around to watch your granddaughter grow up. I don't want to find out you're missing, or see your picture on the front page of a newspaper. Dad, I love you no matter what. But I'm begging you to take a look at your life. It's not too late to change. God can help you."

Carl's father took a long look at Elizabeth and handed her back to Maria. "You need to go now," he said. His voice sounded raspy.

Carl sighed and helped Maria wrap Elizabeth in her pink blanket before they walked out. "I love you, Dad," Carl said.

Carl's dad closed the door, and Carl led his little family toward the car with a heavy heart.

***

Six months before Carl graduated from Atlantic Union College, he still didn't have a job. Once again Carl wondered if perhaps God wanted him to use his engineering degree and be involved with ministry on the side. Unlike many of his fellow classmates, Carl didn't have any connections, and he didn't know anyone who might offer him a position as a pastor of a church.

A surprise phone call from the dean of the college answered Carl's prayer. "There's someone here to visit you," the dean said. "Can you come down?"

A man Carl had never met before introduced himself. "Carl, I hear you have a good head for business and a background with youth. Would you be interested in coming to Orlando, Florida, for a job interview?"

Carl was thrilled at the prospect of working in Florida, doing the job he felt called to do. He wondered how the people from the Florida Conference had found out about him.

"How did they even know about me?" Carl asked the dean when the man was gone.

"I have no idea," the dean answered. "Apparently you were highly recommended by five different sources. There were three names on their list, but they're interested in having you come and pastor their church."

By the time Carl graduated, there was a church position waiting for him in the Florida Keys. He enjoyed his position there, especially working with the youth of the church.

"You really should be a youth director," one of his new friends said. "That's your gift."

Carl laughed. "That's not the first time I've heard that. In fact, my first pastor told me the same thing when I was a teenager."

A couple of years later an opportunity arose for Carl to go back to school, this time at Andrews University, where he would be able to study theology further and take classes that focused specifically on youth ministry.

Well, God, Carl said, *if You open doors, I'll walk through them.*

Carl, Maria, and Elizabeth moved to Michigan, and Carl started school again—one step closer to the calling God had placed on his life so many years before.

Just before final exam week at Andrews University, Carl received a phone call from his mother. Her voice sounded strange, and Carl's stomach tightened in anticipation of what he could only expect to be bad news.

"What is it, Mom?" Carl asked. "What's wrong?"

There was a pause, and it sounded as though his mother was trying to find the right words. "Carl, there's something I need to tell you. It's about your father."

Carl felt his throat tighten. "Is he . . .?"

"He's alive," his mother continued, "but he's in the hospital. He has cancer, Carl. He's dying."

"I'm on my way," he said.

"No, no, don't come now," his mother said. "It's going to be OK. Finish your finals first, and then come."

Carl put down the phone and sat in a daze. So this is how it would end. After all the nights he worried his father would be gunned down in retaliation by a member of a rival crime family or turn up missing in a Mob-related incident, his proud father was now lying in a hospital bed facing the only enemy he had ever battled that he wouldn't be able to defeat: cancer.

Carl could hardly concentrate on his finals knowing his father was fighting for his life back in New York. He couldn't wait to get through the last test and leave for the hospital.

I can talk to him, Carl thought. *Maybe it's not too late. He can still turn his life over to God.*

However, Carl's hopes for one last conversation with his father ended the same week with another phone call from his mother.

"I'm sorry, Carl," his mother said over the phone. "He's gone. Your father is already gone. He just passed away."

It was too late. Carl couldn't hold back the tears as the news sank in. Regret burned a hole through his heart, and he wished he had just forgotten his finals and seized this last opportunity—an opportunity that had evaporated with his father's final breath.

Carl's mother continued. "But there's more you need to know," she said. "Your father was in the same hospital where your aunt works. She talked to him every day while he was there, and she said—"

"Stop, don't tell me any more," Carl said. "If you're going to tell me something about my father, I need to hear it face-to-face."

Within hours of his father's passing, Carl buckled Maria and Elizabeth into the car and began the long trip back to New York. Though his father had been absent for most of his life, Carl felt the loss deeply. As long as his father had been alive, there had also lived a tiny, flickering possibility that God could begin healing the severely damaged bond between them. Now he knew he would never hear his father's voice again, and that thought filled him with a violent storm of anger and sadness.

God! Carl called out silently. His throat ached and tears blurred his eyes as he stared through the windshield at the 721 long miles that lay between him and his childhood home. He gripped the steering wheel with tight fingers. *God, are You even listening? How many years have I begged You to do something to save my father? I've followed You everywhere You've led me. I've listened to You. Now he's gone, and he's going to be lost. I feel as if You betrayed me.*

The voice Carl had become accustomed to hearing was now silent, and Carl was left alone with his thoughts.

CHAPTER 15

The man in the casket surrounded by flowers seemed like a wax shell of the man Carl remembered as his dad. Cancer left Cano Rodriguez thin and brittle, and the lines on his face hinted at the horrors of a dangerous secret life. Yet Carl noticed that there was something strangely peaceful about him. He hardly noticed anyone else was there until his aunt spoke.

"I talked with him every day," Carl's aunt said, coming up behind him as he stood beside the casket. "It was divine appointment that he spent his last days at the hospital where I work as a nurse."

"What do you mean?" Carl said, wiping his eyes.

"This is what your mother was trying to tell you on the phone," his aunt continued gently. "I visited him every day, and I would tell him, 'Cano, the Lord is coming. Your sons are pastors, and they pray for you every day. Don't you want to go to heaven?' But he would tell me to leave him alone."

Carl shook his head. "That sounds like my father."

"But I wouldn't leave him alone. I came in every day. I would go in during my lunch hours and read the Bible to him. And I would say, 'Your kids made a life for themselves the way you wanted them to. You should be proud of them. You missed out on time with your sons in this life, but they want to spend time with you in heaven.' And Carl, he would just cry."

Carl's chest hurt as he listened.

"And then one day," his aunt said, putting her hand on his shoulder, "the day before he died, I came into his room, and he broke down. He said, 'I've lived a bad life. All the things I've done—why would God accept me?' I told him God loved him, and he needed to confess his life to God. He said, 'But I already confessed to a priest in the Catholic Church each time I . . .' And I knew he meant each time he had killed someone for the Mob, 'After each time, I would go to confession.' I told him the Bible says that it doesn't work that way. That it was between him and God, not an earthly priest. I told him that he needed to ask God directly for forgiveness and that God would forgive him. Carl, he cried like a baby. After that," she said, "I saw him at peace. There was a glow. And the next day, he died."

Carl hugged his aunt tightly while the tears washed his cheeks, knowing that his words wouldn't ever be enough to express his gratitude for this amazing woman.

"I'm so thankful for you," Carl said to his aunt. "I've been praying for my father ever since I gave my heart to God, and God was listening the whole time. Thank you for not giving up on my dad."

For Carl, his father's funeral was a mixture of grief and celebration. When his turn came to speak, he stood up and looked down at his father's peaceful face. He was about to begin when he noticed a commotion in the back of the room.

Heads turned as several men in tailored suits entered through the door and stood stiffly near the exit.

Carl recognized at least one of the men and his body-guard. The mood tensed with the arrival of the formidable guests, and the air was heavy.

They're here, Carl thought as he looked at the members of the Mafia with ill-concealed guns that lined the back of the room. *They're here to pay last respects to my father.*

Carl began. "My father died with peace, and I'm going to see him again," Carl said. "I have the hope of heaven, and that's what God wants for you, also. He wants you to be there."

Carl appealed to the people in the room from his heart, not wanting anyone to walk away without the same assurance his father had on his deathbed. Several people came forward, but the hardened-looking men on the back row didn't move.

I'll never have this chance again, Carl thought, suddenly feeling boldness fill his heart. He was surprised that he wasn't afraid about what he planned to do. *I guess I'm just not afraid to die,* Carl thought. *I have something nobody and nothing can ever take away from me, not even death.*

When the service ended, he made his way to the back of the room to face the group of clean-shaven mobsters. He walked up to them unflinching, not caring about the Mob family they represented or the loaded guns resting in their holsters.

"You may be surprised to know this," Carl said, looking each man in the face, "but I'm not sad that my dad is dead. He was a bad man who did bad things."

The men looked directly at Carl while he spoke.

"But you know what?" Carl continued. "My dad

died at peace with God, and he has heaven to look forward to. If you don't make peace with God, the only thing you have to look forward to is punishment for the choices you've made. Wouldn't you rather have peace?"

Some of the men immediately turned and walked out, but a couple of them stayed. One man looked at another man, who looked down at his feet and nodded. Carl could see in their eyes that they knew he was right. He could only imagine what it must be like to lie in bed at night with the constant fear of being erased at the nod of a Mob boss's head, or being haunted by the faces of people they had murdered for money. He hoped that the chance to finally have relief from guilt and peace with God would be enough to inspire them to change.

Carl prayed silently while they deliberated, but eventually the men turned and walked away without saying a word. Carl was disappointed, but he remembered that he had prayed for his dad for years, and he knew that God's timing is always perfect.

God, You are good, he prayed, looking up at the stained-glass picture in the funeral home chapel. *You never let go, even when I pushed You away.*

Carl turned and looked back at his family, thankful that the sad occasion of saying goodbye to his father was tinged with hope and celebration. He knew he would see his father again someday. And they would have a lot to catch up on.

EPILOGUE

Carl Rodriguez is now the youth director for the Chesapeake Conference of Seventh-day Adventists. He is in charge of youth and young adult ministry, including mission trips, summer camps, leadership training, and the Adventurer and Pathfinder clubs. A couple of times per year he also accepts speaking engagements to share his story.

Carl believes with all his heart that when a person commits every aspect of his or her life to God, He fulfills His promises:

"But seek first his kingdom and his righteousness, and all these things will be given to you as well. Therefore do not worry about tomorrow, for tomorrow will worry about itself. Each day has enough trouble of its own" (Matthew 6:33, 34).

"I [Jesus] have come that they may have life, and have it to the full" (John 10:10).

"It's a journey of trust that might take months or even years," Carl says. "But it all comes down to a decision: Do you trust God to lead in your life or not? The sooner you figure that out, the sooner life to the full becomes a reality."

Carl and his wife, Maria, live happily in the country.